As We're Going

*A Journey Toward
Congregation Based
Disciple Making*

Thomas Foley

Christian Educators Outreach

ISBN-13: 978-0-9990542-0-8.

Christian Educators Outreach
Charlottesville, Virginia
www.ceokids.org

The views expressed in this work are those of the author, not necessarily those of Christian Educators Outreach, its Board of Directors or employees.

THESE PERMISSIONS ARE GRATEFULLY ACKNOWLEDGED
Scripture quotations are from the ESV® Bible (The Holy Bible, English Standard Version®), copyright © 2001 by Crossway, a publishing ministry of Good News Publishers. Used by permission. All rights reserved.
THE COLLECTED LETTERS VOL I by C.S. Lewis
copyright © C.S. Lewis Pte. Ltd. 2000.
THE COLLECTED LETTERS VOL II by C.S. Lewis
copyright © C.S. Lewis Pte. Ltd. 2004.
THE FOUR LOVES by C.S. Lewis copyright © C.S. Lewis Pte. Ltd. 1960.
MERE CHRISTIANITY by C.S. Lewis copyright © C.S. Lewis Pte. Ltd. 1942, 1943, 1944, 1952.
THE WEIGHT OF GLORY by C.S. Lewis copyright © C.S. Lewis Pte. Ltd. 1949.
Extracts reprinted by permission.
Jack: A Life of C. S. Lewis by George Sayer, Copyright © 1988, 1994. Published and used by permission of Crossway, a publishing ministry of Good News Publishers, Wheaton, IL 60187, www.crossway.org.
German Pietism During the Eighteenth Century (1973). and The Rise of Evangelical Pietism. (1971) By F. Ernest Stoeffler. Extracts reprinted by permission. Koninklijke Brill, Leiden, Netherlands
A History of Christian Thought, vol. 2, by Gonzalez, Justo. Nashville, TN: Abingdon, 1971. Used by permission. All Rights Reserved

COVER PHOTO:
taken by the author, Happy Valley Park trail in Port Elizabeth, South Africa

To Un Hwa.
My Sweet Anna,
your encouragement and exhortation
have moved me forward these 37 years.
God has used you
to make me a better disciple
than I could have been without you.
Thank You

Every person wishes to be heard, understood, and valued;
this should be a basic function of disciple making,
how else can we shine the gospel into lives?

CONTENTS

PART THREE
BEING AND MAKING

APPENDICES

PREFACE

While recently reorganizing my study, I discovered and glanced through journals and notebooks that go back a couple of decades. I realized that on my journey of the last 30 years, I've thought and prayed often about a kind of malaise among too many Christians, what John Stott aptly described as "superficiality."[1] I'm convinced that disciple making is the answer to that superficiality. It then dawned on me, this little book has been a long time in the making.

I focused on the apparent absence of disciple making and reflected on what can be done at the congregational level. Disciple making *should* draw followers of Jesus into an ever-deepening relationship with Him, producing fruitful, godly lives. That is my aim.

It should be noted that this work is written from a decidedly low ecclesiological perspective. But I submit that the ideas and suggestions would be helpful to someone holding a higher ecclesiology as well. Disciple making is a command of Jesus. Indeed, I argue that disciple making should be the major focus of all congregations and will naturally result in duplication. Therefore, this work may be called missional. It has also been suggested that this is a paradigm shift. But, I prefer to think it is a return to an earlier model. It is my hope that this work will inform leaders across cultures and up and down all varieties of church perspectives. It was with the intent to inform leaders that I researched and wrote. Thus, I have sought answers from Jesus, Scripture, and Christian history.

I fully understand that my premises and conclusions will not be met with agreement by all readers. Some will completely disagree. It is a limited work and, I'm sure, will be called lopsided. That's perfectly fine. But by disagreeing with me as you read, I have actually succeeded because thinking has been fostered. Sometimes disagreement can be the midwife of further understanding. Helping someone gain a better understanding of biblical disciple making will be a great victory for me. Even if, especially if, it

---

[1] John Stott, *The Radical Disciple: Some Neglected Aspects of Our Calling* (Downers Grove, IL: InterVarsityPress, 2012), kindle, location 278.

originates with disagreement. Thus, my aim is to inform and, maybe, inspire, or at least to provoke. Whatever the case, may fresh thought prevail and may disciple making be the result.

In an attempt to make this work accessible, it has been kept small in scope. The chapters here are more numerous and smaller than the dissertation that was its forerunner. (I've also found and fixed numerous errors from that text in this version – no doubt you too, will find more errors of numerous kinds, but I hope not too many). Knowing this began as an academic work, one associate asked if it is going to be readable. Well, that remains to be seen and each reader will have to be the judge. If you classify it as 'not well written' – well, that's on me, and me alone.

A colleague encouraged me to go hunting for a publisher. After consideration, I decided that Christian Educators Outreach (CEO) would be the best publisher. In this way, CEO produces its first ministry resource and should there be any proceeds from the sale of the book, those resources will go to CEO. Let me also, at this point, say that these are my views, not necessarily the views of CEO, our Board, employees or colleagues. But I hope they will be.

You'll find that, after some debate about footnotes verses endnotes, I kept the footnotes. Like me, many are interested in seeing the source without having to go hunting. I also used the footnotes to add information that would not interrupt the flow of the text but may be of interest to some readers. There are also some comments about resources that may be helpful should the reader wish to learn more about a given topic.

In the end, I hope the reader will consider this disciple making model, a model that I have seen God use to make disciples in numerous contexts. I hope the reader will adapt, adjust and attune what is presented. Thus, I hope, whether you argue or agree, disciple making will begin, or become more effective in producing fruitful, godly disciples of Jesus. So, *as we're going* let's obey Jesus and make disciples.

ACKNOWLEDGEMENTS

This resource is the result of my doctoral thesis. I'm thankful that this work of joy was encouraged by the board of Christian Educators Outreach. They, led at that time by Janice Carter, encouraged me by reminding me (as we discussed whether should I do the doctoral program or not) that our middle name is Educators. They (as did my wife, Anna) understood the value of pursuing a doctoral program before I did. I'm grateful for Dr. Peter Kuzmič who urged me to start and especially for the thousands of pages he and Dr. Kevin Xiyi Yao gave me to read in the program. That reading was meaningful to ponder and greatly influenced this work.

I have deep gratitude for my supporters, who pray for me and give generously to our work, without whom I could not travel to preach, mentor, coach, and make disciples.

I thank God for my fellow disciples in numerous time zones who have taught me about being a disciple and making disciples as we walked together (especially the 333 club who urged me forward weekly for three years).

As far as thanks for those who have discipled me, I must give thanks to God for Dave Schwartz, who, in many ways modeled disciple making for me even before I believed. I'm grateful for Robert Alderman who pastored and discipled me in my early years as a Christian minister. He modeled disciple making for me as he mentored me personally and professionally.

I'm grateful for the library staff at Alderman Library at the University of Virginia, for my daughter, Joanna Luper, who found obscure books and articles at the Liberty University library, and for those who read early drafts and excerpts and challenged my ideas, especially for Serhiy Bogachuk and for Peter Hrechkosiy (and Anna Kinal and Olga Yatsentiuk whose translation of early versions of Part Three into Ukrainian made that counsel possible), for Bill Copeland, Mark Frazier, Jeff Bloxsom and Eric Goetz, I thank God for their suggestions and urging, and for Dr. Kevin Xiyi Yao, who encouraged me that I could, especially that day when I was no longer sure. I express my gratitude for Luke Davis, who helped me see, post oral defense, how a new chapter arrangement would help the flow. I'm thankful for the thesis reading team in the Doctor of Ministry office at Gordon-Conwell Theological Seminary who gave me so many helpful suggestions, for all these, I give praise to God.

I am especially thankful for Dr. Roger Munsick who challenged everything and read every word - several times. In many ways, Roger really was my doctoral mentor. For all these and my fellow disciples in seven nations who didn't get specific mention, but are at the heart of this work, and whose ministries were foremost in mind as I wrote, for you all, I am grateful to God.

I am grateful for family, our daughters Joanna and Rebecca and their husbands, Will and Leland (two of the greatest gifts God could give a dad, men who love God first). I'm thankful to God for the fresh insight into life that our three grandsons, William, Alexander and Wyatt have given me, just by being here they make me want to go on. But, most significant of them all, I express enormous gratitude for my dear wife Anna, who has pushed, prodded, exhorted, encouraged, and sacrificed. She is used by our heavenly Father every day of my life to teach me about being a student of Jesus.

Finally, in this, the 500th year of the Reformation, I remember that God gets all the glory, and for His empowering of this project I give thanks. I give this work to Him to use as He wills, for His will is always good.

Tom Foley
Charlottesville
June 2017

INTRODUCTION

In a small city in Eastern Europe an evangelical church struggles along. Last week there were thirty persons present in the weekly service, the week before thirty-two, this week twenty-six. This attendance sometimes jumps up to 45 and the little building is full. This happens whenever there is a special event or when humanitarian aid is delivered. The pastor is in his thirties with a wife and three primary school age children. They struggle by with monthly financial support from two churches in England and one in Canada. Italian churches send the humanitarian aid. The description of life in this little church is not greatly different than it would have been when the first missionary arrived here in the 1990s, little has changed. Once a year a team of about eight people arrives from the United States to 'do outreach.' Every year, they visit the main square of the city to perform skits and pass out flyers for an English program. This is how they advertise the English club at the church they will participate in. Every year they spend their two-week trip teaching English and playing games with twenty or so primary aged children. On the last night of the English club, pizza is ordered and soft drinks are brought in. The worship band leads singing, certificates are passed out for completing the English program. The pastor gives a brief evangelistic message. Afterward, everyone enjoys pizza, cookies, and ice cream. Then everyone goes home. On Sunday, there are only fifteen in church because the Americans have left and everyone is exhausted. None of the visitors return.

This story is fictitious. The elements of our little story, however, are not mythical. They are based on reality. I could describe dozens of real stories just like this in towns in many cultures. In America, the story is a little different, they probably do not have the mission team. Or, if they do, they would be fixing up houses, or the church itself, as young people from middle class congregations load up in vans and travel to neighboring states to help congregations that are less well off. The churches to which these servants come may be larger than in our story, but the attendance result is the same flat trend. The instances that we describe are the result of what some call the attractional method. A model that is based on attracting people to a place, an event. Let's have an event, invite the neighborhood kids, feed them pizza or tacos or cook hot dogs and get them to a service so that we can preach the gospel to them and their parents. We think: as long as they hear, we've done all we can. When things quiet down, we schedule another event. And another. And another. I know this well. You see, at some level, I have been the pastor, and I have led that mission team.

Through years of observation and discussion with pastors, I concluded that there was something fundamentally wrong in these stories. There is a lack of depth. I see the pastors struggle and churches fade. My response is to invest in the leaders themselves more than their churches. I make the case for spiritual growth through the disciplines. In some places, real progress is made. I have seen the value in working with fellow disciples. For years, I have invested in as many leaders as possible, urging them to grow deep in Christ. For years, we used the word discipleship without really knowing what we meant. From these experiences emerged the vision for this project that seeks to explore some important questions. These question stem from the assertion of church leaders that there is a lack of discipleship in the church. What is this widely used word 'discipleship?' How does it differ from disciple making? What does Scripture teach us? What can history teach us? What may we learn from Jesus and His disciples? Why did disciple making exist so sacrificially, and then appear to fade? Why is it largely missing today and what can be done to correct the problem? Leaders of smaller congregations want a concise model for disciple making, where is it? This project culminates by proposing a simple, adaptable, duplicatable model of congregational based disciple making.

PART ONE

EXPLORING DISCIPLE MAKING:

THE LACK, THE WORDS AND THE SOURCE

CHAPTER ONE

OVERCOMING
SUPERFICIAL CHRISTIANITY

Early in the second century, Ignatius of Antioch (c.35 - c.110), a leader of Christian churches, was forcibly removed from the city where he served and taken to Rome. He was to be executed as a Christian martyr. Along the way, he noted personal mistreatment by the soldiers who were charged with his transport. In this context, he did some letter writing, including what it meant to him to be a disciple. "Now I begin to be a disciple … Let fire and cross, flocks of beasts, broken bones, dismemberment … come upon me, so long as I attain to Jesus Christ."[1] Not long after he penned these words, Ignatius was put to death for his faith in Jesus. K. H. Rengstorf notes that "Ignatius can say that only the martyr is a true disciple."[2] This may be a paraphrase of his words, but Ignatius' point is made through his testimony more than through his verbal expressions. Ignatius paid the ultimate price and proved himself a disciple. These are among the earliest teachings after the Bible on what it means to be a disciple. At that time, in the very early church, there was a great cost to being a disciple. Those who have studied the early history of the Christians understand that it was a challenging time as many of them were put to death for their faith. Such was the situation for so many in the first 300 years of the Church.

Nearly two millennia later, things are very different for many churches, especially in the West. Dallas Willard, influential Evangelical philosopher and former professor at the University of Southern California, laments that many Christians might be "willing to die but obviously are not

---

[1] Christian History, "Ignatius of Antioch," ChristianityToday.com, http://www.christianitytoday.com/history/people/martyrs/ignatius-of-antioch.html (accessed May 31, 2016).

[2] K. H. Rengstorf, "*mathánō*." in *Theological Dictionary of the New Testament*, ed. Gerhard Kittel and Gerhard Friedrich, trans., abr. ed., ed., Geoffrey W. Bromiley (Grand Rapids: Eerdmans Publishing, 1985), 562.

ready to live, and can hardly get along with themselves, much less others."[3] Willard refers to a weakness in the general Christian population. This project investigates the lack of mature disciples (students) of Jesus and proposes a solution.

Converts or Maturing Christians?

Many Christian leaders around the world join Willard and warn that the greater Church is, as has been widely stated, a mile wide and an inch deep. In his final book, John Stott declares: "There is superficiality of discipleship everywhere, and church leaders bemoan this situation."[4] He recounts how, in the 1990's, he had spoken frequently about the global church's "'growth without depth.'"[5] This problem is wide, but it is not new.

Scripture is replete with admonitions to 'hold on' and not drift away, *to grow in maturity* instead of remaining stagnant. Nowhere is this clearer than in the New Testament letter to the Hebrews. The writer states that his readers "ought to be teachers"[6] yet they still need the "basic principles of the oracles of God."[7] The writer then clarifies his meaning. "You need milk, not solid food, for everyone who lives on milk is unskilled in the word of righteousness, since he is a child."[8] He addresses his readers as immature believers. The writer then explains that solid food "is for the mature, for those who have their powers of discernment trained by constant practice to distinguish good from evil."[9] From the letter to the Hebrews we see that the was concern about immaturity. It is noteworthy that Stott's twenty-first century concern of superficiality existed among the leaders of the first century.

Today, as then, there is the danger of immature believers. We may even assert that too many congregations are largely populated by parishioners

---

[3] Willard, *The Great Omission* (New York, HarperCollins, 2006), 69.

[4] John Stott, *The Radical Disciple: Some Neglected Aspects of Our Calling* (Downers Grove, IL: InterVarsityPress, 2012), kindle location 282.

[5] Stott, *Radical Disciple*, loc. 278.

[6] Hebrews 5:12. The Holy Bible, English Standard Version® (ESV®) Copyright © 2001 by Crossway, a publishing ministry of Good News Publishers. All rights reserved. ESV Text Edition: 2016

[7] Hebrews 5:12.

[8] Hebrews 5:12-13.

[9] Hebrews 5:14.

whose faith has grown little from the place it began. Paul warned Timothy against putting new converts[10] in leadership. These converts may be thought of as immature believers. Their level of maturity is without regard to the number of years they have attended Christian gatherings. They are caring and kind people who dutifully join others for pleasantries, worshipful music and an inspiring sermon each Sunday. They may serve on committees and work in the soup kitchen, yet many rarely experience real gospel-centered change and seldom seek to learn, and radically obey the teachings of Jesus. Their commitment level is low as observed when things don't go their way. For them, prayer is something done in church, during difficulties or something that the clergy does as a part of their duties. When things in the congregation don't proceed as they think they should, they may move to another church, or worse, stop gathering with other believers altogether. Stott assesses the cause of the problem as noted earlier when he stated the Church suffers from "growth without depth."[11]

Is Church Growth at the Root of the Problem?

The assertion that the global church is largely failing to create maturing Christians, particularly from such a highly respected evangelical leader, is an indictment that carries great weight and demands a thoughtful and biblical response. Stott's conclusion is correct. We may also assert that this lack of depth within the congregants is, largely, not their fault. This project asserts that this weakness results from years of emphasis on proclamation-based church growth programs. The focus of these programs is usually numerical growth rather than spiritual depth. Too many church members suffer from a lack of the most basic theological understanding.

---

[10] 'Convert' is an adjective used only once in the New Testament. In 1 Timothy 3:6 Paul uses the adjective νεόφυτον (*neophutos): "lit. newly planted*" - Walter Bauer, *A Greek-English Lexicon of the New Testament and Other Early Christian Literature*, ed. Frederick W. Danker, 2nd ed. (Chicago: University of Chicago Press, 1979), 536.). Paul warns against giving church responsibility to weak believers. Similarly, he referred to the struggling church in Corinth: "But I, brothers, could not address you as spiritual people, but as people of the flesh, as infants in Christ. (1 Cor. 3:1) When we consider this concept in light of our stated problem of "inch deep Christians" we see an old problem that lingers today.

[11] Stott, *Radical Disciple*, location 278.

Robert Coleman states the case plainly about the church growth issue.

> Too quickly is this issue passed over in church growth discussions, even within the Evangelical community. Much of what is said on this subject comes largely from sociological and behavioristic research, not the content of the Christian Mission. The result is that interest turns primarily to humanistic consideration, like more astute communication techniques or better institutional programs.[12]

With this assertion in mind, the question emerges: How can a local congregation foster maturing believers? The answer to that foundational question will propel us through all that follows.

Lines of Inquiry

To seek the answer to such a question, this project explores many other questions. What is a biblical understanding of discipleship? What is the difference between 'discipleship' and 'disciple making'?[13] What is the importance of disciple making in advancing God's Kingdom? One avenue of inquiry within this project is the etymology of the Greek verb *mathēteusate (make disciples)*, the only imperative verb in Matthew 28:19.[14] These questions guide us through Chapter Two.

How is *mathēteusate* a key to *Missio Dei* (mission of God)? To answer this, we turn to our master, Jesus. We specifically examine His method and the role of question asking in Chapter Four. We will especially focus on what may be learned from His method as recorded in the Synoptic Gospels. It is important to understand Jesus' context as a disciple maker, therefore in Chapter Five we will examine key aspects of disciple making in His historical context. Further, we consider the effect of Socratic Method on the Rabbis of

---

[12] Robert E. Coleman, *The Master Plan of Discipleship* (Old Tappan, N.J.: Fleming H. Revell Co., 1987), p. 143.

[13] Throughout this exploration, we will use the term 'disciple making' that is inspired by the Greek verb μαθητεύσατε which is often translated 'make disciples' in modern English translations. We will explore the nuances of this word in the next chapter.

[14] The reader is reminded that the Great Commission is not just about foreign missions. It is a mandate for all disciples. Everywhere. Until He returns.

the era surrounding Jesus. This study of the context preceding and during the ministry of and preceding Jesus are in Chapter Six.

Since Christian history is a record of the following of the Great Commission, we look to history and ask why discipleship existed so sacrificially in the early church only, apparently, to fade? That inquiry guides Part Two. We examine the Desert Fathers, Augustine, Thomas Aquinas, Luther, Calvin, Spener, C. S. Lewis and others bringing our study from the First to the Twentieth centuries.

The practical application of the research will be considered in how one may mature as a disciple through practices in personal discipleship, the subject of Part Three. Also, in the third section we come full circle to disciple making, the imperative of the Great Commission, with what we call a Congregation Based Disciple Making Method. This method is explained beginning in Chapter Fifteen and will complete the proposal of a simple model for disciple making.

Biblical, Duplicatable and Culturally Adaptable

This entire exploration has, as its practical outcome one objective: to demonstrate a biblical, duplicatable, and (largely) culturally adaptable model for disciple making. Success in this endeavor will enable leaders to better understand the problem. With that understanding in mind, a positive outcome will be disciple-makers in congregations who are motivated and equipped and will lead others to make disciples. To that end this inquiry begins through exploring several important terms: disciple, discipleship and disciple making, this exploration will be the focus of Chapter Two.

Questions for Understanding

At the end of each chapter of this project, the reader will find several questions to help foster further understanding. Knowledge is only the first, and sometimes a shallow, step. To pause and understand is key to producing a positive outcome in growth in maturity. These questions will be applicative in nature. It is hoped that the reader will pause and think about the question as much as trying to answer them. Learning about questions and developing the skill of asking good questions, as we will see, is an important skill in disciple making.

Applicative Questions

What do you think of when you hear the word 'discipleship?' What has been the best definition of 'disciple' that has helped you?

If you were to describe an immature believer, what adjectives or synonyms would you think of?

A person who has attended a congregation for many years comes up to you and asks you to help them grow as a disciple of Jesus. What are the strategies you would use to help them move in that direction?

CHAPTER TWO

DISCIPLESHIP AND DISCIPLE MAKING

In 1549, the English reformer Hugh Latimer (c.1485-1555[1]) preached a sermon to the court of King Edward VI. Latimer was a key figure in the English Reformation and was known for his preaching. He frequently preached at the royal court where, in a sermon, Latimer uses the word discipleship. This is, per the Oxford English Dictionary, the first recorded use of the word 'discipleship' in English.[2] It was used by a preacher who would be become one of the Oxford Martyrs.[3] If this word is used in a sermon in the royal court, certainly it had become familiar to the hearers. Thus, the word has at least a 500-year history in English. But upon careful reflection, the term 'discipleship' lacks precision. This is particularly notable because it is so frequently used in Christian ministry and literature today. Indeed, we assert that the word is somewhat ambiguous.

What Do We Mean by Discipleship?

Many books and journal articles are published annually on the subject of discipleship.[4] One volume on discipleship may sound like a book on spiritual development, another like a manual for church growth,[5] while a third may be a mixture of the two promoting a certain conference or curriculum.[6] Other works on the subject focus on grace and/or balance and are to be

---

[1] *Encyclopedia of Protestantism*, 2004 ed., s.v. "Hugh Latimer" by Deborah K. Marcuse.

[2] *Oxford English Dictionary*, 2nd. ed. s.v. "discipleship."

[3] Latimer, like Ignatius of Antioch before him, would die for his faith when Edward VI was succeeded on England's throne by Roman Catholic Mary. Mary's administration had no tolerance for Protestants like Latimer.

[4] An Amazon.com search on June 10, 2016 listed over one thousand titles on the subject.

[5] Dave Early and Rod Dempsey, *Disciple Making Is* (Nashville: B&H Academic, 2013).

[6] Randy Pope, *Insourcing* (Grand Rapids: Zondervan, 2013).

found on the bookshelf next to volumes that read like management guides.[7] Thus, it follows that a clearer understanding of the word itself is important. What does 'discipleship' mean?

The *Oxford English Dictionary* states that 'discipleship' is the condition or task of a disciple.[8] The definition is derived by adding the suffix '-ship,' meaning to embody "a quality or state,"[9] to the word 'disciple' creating the noun 'discipleship.' A further complicating question is whether one intends to use the verb or the noun form of 'disciple?' In the search for clarity, research takes us from Latimer in a 1549 sermon to a 2016 podcast in which influential Evangelical leader John Piper notes that the word is not used in the Bible. Further, he asserts the English term is vague.[10] He states that discipleship may refer to one's own system of disciplines. In this instance, Piper refers to the state of being a disciple, thus the noun form, for example: "I am a disciple of Jesus." This would probably be the way that many books have as their underlying philosophy: developing one's own life of following Jesus, considering every aspect of one's life.

The second type is based on the verb use; I might say "I disciple pastors in my network of leaders in seven countries." Piper explained that, in this case, 'discipleship' can mean one's process of making disciples.[11] His assertion that the term contains ambiguities is correct. Thus, the term is both ambiguous and ubiquitous. In this project, because of this apparent lack of clarity about the etymology and usage of 'discipleship,' a more biblically based term will be used generally. To that end, we turn to a key rendering of the Great Commission. This project asserts that the Matthean 'Great

---

[7] For a helpful description of the various 'discipleship' models, see Michael Wilkins, *Following the Master: A Biblical Theology of Discipleship* (Grand Rapids, MI: Zondervan Publishing Co., 1992), 11-21. Wilkins has a model of his own and that model, of course, influences his assertions, but the description is very helpful nonetheless.

[8] OED, "discipleship."

[9] MerriamWebster.com, s.v. "-ship," "something showing, exhibiting, or embodying a quality or state <township> <fellowship> - -", http://www.merriam-webster.com/dictionary/-ship (accessed 24 May 2016).

[10] John Piper, "What is Discipleship and How is It Done?" (podcast) posted January 25, 2016, http://www.desiringgod.org/interviews/what-is-discipleship-and-how-is-it-done (accessed 24 May 2016). By John Piper. © Desiring God Foundation. Source: *desiringGod.org*.

[11] Piper, "What is Discipleship."

Commission' (28:19) is *the* mandate for the Church. The argument presented here hinges on the Greek imperative verb μαθητεύσατε (*mathēteusate*) which is translated 'make disciples' in most modern English translations.[12]

'Disciple Making'

Our inquiry takes us next to its root word, 'disciple' (μαθητεύω, *mathēteuō*). New Testament scholar Robert Mounce explains. "The Greek verb *mathēteuō* means 'to make a learner' (coming, as it does, from *manthanō* 'to learn')."[13] Mounce further clarifies. "A disciple is not simply one who has been taught but one who continues to learn."[14] Thus to understand the word disciple we may simply state that a disciple is a continuous learner or, perhaps better, a lifelong learner. To think that one has completed his learning, is both a prideful misconception about one's self and a failure to understand the word disciple.

This idea of continuous or lifelong learning is key to this exploration. Ancient text expert K. H. Rengstorf, writing in the *Theological Dictionary of the New Testament,* states that the Greek word *manthanō* means "to be or become a pupil."[15] At the end of the article exploring the uses of *manthanō* (disciple) and its derivatives, he elaborates on the odd little word (*mathēteusate*) that Matthew recorded. "In a distinctive transitive use (Mt. 13:52; 28:19; Acts 14:21) the New Testament also uses the term for 'to make disciples.'"[16] Thus, at this introductory point, we might understand that *mathēteusate* means "to facilitate continuous learners." With that, we turn to our focus to scholarship specifically regarding Matthew's use of *mathēteusate* (make disciples),' or as will be frequently referred to in this project, 'disciple making.'[17]

---

[12] "Go therefore and make disciples of all nations..." (Matthew 28:19).

[13] Robert H. Mounce, *Matthew, New International Biblical Commentary* (Peabody, MA: Hendrickson Publishers, 1985), 268.

[14] Mounce, *Matthew,* 268.

[15] K. H. Rengstorf, "*mathánō.*" in *Theological Dictionary of the New Testament,* ed. Gerhard Kittel and Gerhard Friedrich, trans., abr. ed., ed., Geoffrey W. Bromiley (Grand Rapids: Eerdmans Publishing, 1985), 562.

[16] Rengstorf, s.v. "*mathánō,*" in *Theological Dictionary,* 562.

[17] 'Disciple making' is from the heart of Matthew 28:19 as juxtaposed to the more general term 'discipleship;' 'disciple making' clarifies Jesus' mandate.

Does Proclamation Alone Fulfill or Truncate the Great Commission?

It has already been suggested that the weakness of the church may be a result of a proclamation-based, church growth method. In his work on the Gospel of Matthew, missionary and theologian Frederick Bruner asserts that "the *usual* missionary terms are not employed here: 'preach,' 'convert,' win,..."[18] He also clarifies that the word has equivalency in the "modern-English terms, to 'mentor,' to 'apprentice.'"[19] Bruner's emphasis is rightly focused on one's commitment to obeying Jesus in an ongoing fashion as His disciple. Obeying Jesus' Great Commission, therefore, means being committed to engaging in disciple making. Regarding such a commitment, R. T. France, once Principal of Wycliffe Hall, Oxford, asserts that the level of commitment a disciple must have is *not* satisfied by simply hearing and believing [emphasis mine]. He states that disciples "must also respond with the same wholehearted commitment which was required of those who became disciples of Jesus during his ministry."[20] France points out that being a disciple is a response to a calling and the committed life that follows. This is less like a two-stage process, believe and follow, than it is the first *two steps* on a life-long journey. Hence living as a disciple is not just a static life following a conversion experience or especially that of pursuing a cultural tradition.[21] Juxtapose a comfortable cultural Christianity to Ignatius' assertion: "only the martyr is a true disciple."[22] The discontinuity is evident; the result is a weaker Christianity. One does not die for that to which one is not fully committed. We may then assert that this full commitment to *being a disciple* of Jesus does not usually develop from simply hearing a proclamation and believing. Thus, it is asserted here that proclamation alone truncates the Great Commission.

---

[18] Frederick Dale Bruner, *Matthew: A Commentary, Vol. 2* (Grand Rapids, MI: Eerdmans Publishing Co, 1990), 815.

[19] Bruner, *Matthew*, 815.

[20] R. T. France, *The Gospel of Matthew*, New International Commentary on the New Testament (Grand Rapids, MI: Eerdmans Publishing Co., 2007), 1115.

[21] 'Cultural' is used herein as widely as in a country like Croatia where Roman Catholicism is deeply engrained in the culture to make attendance at mass 'the thing to do' or as narrowly as a family of Virginia Baptists taking their adolescent children to church against their will because that is the way they were 'raised.'

[22] Rengstorf, s.v. "*mathánō*," in *Theological Dictionary*, 562.

France further asserts that proclamation is simply the means to an end. The objective is not that people would simply hear but that they would become disciples. He states that the great "commission is expressed not in terms of the means, to proclaim the good news, but of the end, to 'make disciples.'"[23] Thus, we may see that there has been something very close to putting the ecclesiastical cart before the theological horse. When church growth rather than disciple making is the end in mind, and proclamation becomes the actual end, the Greek imperative and indicative in Matthew 28:19-20 have been reversed. France continues. "The sentence structure is of a main verb in the imperative, 'make disciples,' followed by two uncoordinated participles, 'baptizing' and 'teaching,' which spell out the process of making disciples."[24] Thus to baptize and to teach is Jesus' outline for how to make disciples.

France is not alone; others have rebutted the idea that the imperative is simply to preach and win converts. New Testament professor Douglas Hare argues that "the most remarkable feature of Matthew's commissioning statement is the absence of any call to preach the gospel!"[25] One might conclude, following Hare, that proclamation is secondary. One may wish to relegate preaching and even a congregation's regular weekly gathering to a status of lower importance to mentoring or coaching. But this would be an unbiblical *overemphasis*. We are *commanded* to proclaim the gospel. Indeed, teaching *is* one of the indicatives that Jesus commands in Matthew 28:19-20 and is an important function of fulfilling the Great Commission.[26] However, there is a danger that a great preaching and teaching ministry simply fills buildings with seekers and immature believers who are satisfied with the state of their growth. They are not, in this condition, *committed to growing* "in the

---

[23] France, *The Gospel of Matthew*, 1115.

[24] France, *The Gospel of Matthew*, 1115.

[25] Douglas Hare, *Matthew: Interpretation: A Bible Commentary for Teaching and Preaching* (Louisville Kentucky: Westminster John Knox Press, 1993), 334.

[26] It is important to note, at this juncture, that in this project, cross-cultural ministry is the mortar that holds together the different bricks of this exploration and assertion. The author contends that in its truest sense, the cross-cultural nature of the Great Commission has the same applicability to a central Virginia college town as to a southern Hungary college town. 'As you go' means where you are. This idea of 'as you go' is the basis for our title: *As We're Going.*

15

grace and knowledge of our Lord and Savior Jesus Christ."[27] This proclamation emphasis without actual disciple making may accurately be described a truncation of the Great Commission because it has lessened the impact of Jesus' Commission.

British apologist Michael Green boldly asserts that Jesus called for more than just making converts. "Matthew is not satisfied, Jesus is not satisfied with any hasty profession of faith, any perfunctory baptism. The apostles are called not to evoke decisions but to make disciples."[28] Green rightly reminds the reader that the disciple is to respond to Jesus' call to *be* His disciple and participate in the development of others. This ongoing, lifelong process is what this project calls disciple making.

Disciple Making Conversations

At this juncture, we assert the biblical role of the congregational gathering is for preaching and teaching in disciple making. Disciples are spiritually fed and challenged from the pulpit. But it is asserted here that teaching and preaching should work in concert with disciples who meet regularly for mutual encouragement and exhortation. Biblical and theological truths are best applied around a table where 'fellow disciples'[29] discuss Scripture through honest, regular and vulnerable conversations. These conversations focus on Scripture, are guided by good questions, and point one another to Christ. These tables are where natural conversations take place. It could be a breakfast, lunch or dinner table. It could be in a restaurant, cafe or pub. The location of this table is not as important as the disciple making conversation that takes place.[30] Experience suggests, even demands, that preaching and teaching alone run the risk of enabling Christians to remain immature believers. Rather, an important work of local congregations is to nurture believers into fruitful disciples.

---

[27] 2 Peter 3:18.

[28] Michael Green, *Matthew for Today: Expository Study of Matthew* (Dallas, Texas: Word Publishing, 1988), 322.

[29] The term 'fellow disciples' will be used throughout this investigation. The term describes a collaborative approach to disciple making rather than a mentor - protégé model where the more experienced disciple becomes the discipler (or 'master') of the less experienced. In this work, the collaborative model focuses *all* 'fellow disciples' upon Jesus as their master.

[30] This model will be further explained in Part Three.

Donald Hagner, Professor Emeritus of New Testament at Fuller Seminary, states that Matthew's Great Commission is a call to "... the arduous task of nurturing [persons] into the experience of discipleship" and "to follow after righteousness as articulated in the teaching of Jesus."[31] Hagner's twofold assertion is clear: first, we nurture others which, second, helps them into obedience to Jesus. This nurturing process is often not as easy as one might hope, either in the time it takes or in how the process develops. Indeed, when one reads the Gospels, Jesus would teach and reteach (and reteach) his disciples. They followed Him, but often with a lack of understanding. This presents an important lesson for disciple makers. We must not be in too much of a hurry in the process, patience is key to nurturing.

Jesus is the perfect model of patience. Among the many examples of this in the Gospels is the occasion of His entry to Jerusalem. At the end of the incident John notes that they "...did not understand these things...",[32] yet Jesus persevered with them. Green reminds us. "Matthew has shown throughout his book how slow Jesus' disciples were to do what he wanted."[33] Our Lord provides us with a wonderful example of patience and flexibility. Patience with others in the disciple making process is critical, yet difficult. The commitment to follow Jesus' call requires energy, time and perseverance. To nurture 'fellow disciples' is hard work, but *it is the imperative* of the Great Commission.

Considering the cost of that worthy investment is important to our inquiry. All investments have an initial outlay, investing in people is no different. God paid a high price for His investment in us. Leon Morris explains. "Jesus' disciples are people for whom a life has been given in ransom (Matthew 20:28)[34] and who are committed to the service of the master, who not only took time to teach his disciples but who died for them and rose again."[35] This is the sacrificial commitment of Jesus to the community he is establishing, a community of sacrificial disciples, fellow disciples.

---

[31] Donald A. Hagner, *Word Biblical Commentary, Volume 33A, Matthew 14-28* (Dallas, Texas: Word Books, 1995), 887.

[32] John 12:16.

[33] Green, *Matthew for Today*, 322.

[34] "...even as the Son of Man came not to be served but to serve, and to give his life as a ransom for many." Matthew 20:28.

[35] Leon Morris, *The Gospel According to Matthew* (Grand Rapids Michigan: William B. Eerdmans Publishing Company. 1992), 746.

As disciples enter the community of fellow learners, the process must be intentionally ongoing. Craig Blomberg states that this growth "does not stop after someone makes a profession of faith."[36] Indeed, this is only the first step. Disciple making is best understood as journeying together in the spirit of Paul's letter to his beloved Ephesus. In this epistle, walking together is a key theme. Walking is the nature of the journey after its beginning. Lesslie Newbigin concurs when he argues that discipleship is a calling rather than "a two-stage affair in which a concept of truth is first formulated and is then translated into a program for action. It is a single action of faith and obedience to a living person, the response to a personal calling."[37] Newbigin may be understood to say that true disciple making is the natural stride of walking with others behind Jesus in "faith and obedience."[38] While evangelism is a *critical* component of the Great Commission, it is only the first step in the journey of investing in one another's growth throughout a life of following Jesus. Yet, we are faced with many congregations who have not made disciples and we must consider the challenge of their becoming disciple-makers. Evangelism is incomplete without disciple making that, to be biblical, must follow naturally, step by step on the lifelong journey of following Jesus. It is to Him that we turn, seeking a kind of plumb line of disciple making. So, we look next to the Master.

Applicative Questions

How would you describe your feeling as you read the assertions that preaching alone truncates the Great Commission?

Think back to your own beginning as a Christian, did someone invest personal time with you helping you grow in grace and knowledge of Jesus?

---

[36] Craig L. Blomberg, *Matthew: An Exegetical and Theological Exposition of Holy Scripture*, The New American Commentary, Volume 23 (Nashville, TN: Broadman Publishers, 1992), 431.

[37] Lesslie Newbigin, *Proper Confidence: Faith, Doubt, and Certainty in Christian Discipleship* (Grand Rapids Michigan: William B. Eerdmans Publishing Company, 1995), 66.

[38] Newbigin, *Proper Confidence*, 66.

CHAPTER THREE

TOWARD A MODEL OF DISCIPLE MAKING:
LOOKING TO JESUS

We have argued that many of today's great challenges within congregations, and in the broader church, stem from the fact that there are too many undeveloped disciples. In his landmark work, *The Master Plan of Evangelism*, a call for disciple making, William Coleman bemoans the lack of disciple making today. He asserts that in our age of megachurches, there is "emphasis on numbers of converts, candidates for baptism, and more members for the church, with little or no genuine concern...."[1] for the people themselves. A church growth method that places an undue emphasis on proclamation alone results in a weakened congregation. Many leaders now realize this problem and seek a deeper life in union with God for themselves and for those they lead. Dallas Willard notes that a growing interest exists in spiritual formation.[2] He warns against the practical irrelevance of weak congregations, yet he gives hope that change is afoot. It is clear upon reading Willard, that spiritual formation is an answer to Coleman's call. We will return to the idea of spiritual formation in Chapter Thirteen and consider Willard's influence.

Learning from and Adapting Jesus' Method

Certainly, an exploration of Jesus' methods of disciple making are crucial to our understanding. From the methods of Jesus, we learn lessons that we can apply and adapt to our 21st century contexts. But our lessons are merely applications of His methods. James Dunn, a British New Testament scholar, asserts that our methods today are but imitations of how discipleship

---

[1] Robert Coleman, *The Master Plan of Evangelism* (Grand Rapids, MI: Revell Publishing Co, 1993), Kindle ed., 32.
[2] Dallas Willard, *Renovation of the Heart* (Colorado Springs, CO: NavPress, 2002), 20.

was accomplished in first century Galilee.[3] We cannot expect to be just like Jesus, but we can learn from His lessons and adapt and emulate His method. Dunn asserts that the development of our practices must to be adapted "from the record of those who literally followed him, otherwise such claims to discipleship can easily become fanciful and subject to distorting pressures from tradition and ecclesiastical vested interest.[4]" We draw from Jesus in developing our methods. Sometimes we do this in the face of pressure from others to produce numerical results quickly. Rather, we study Jesus to apply his lessons and bring us to a biblical model of relationships rather than a scheme that may be handed down from a denomination. Dunn's comment about the vested interest of church hierarchies is telling. These pressures to achieve some organizational metric are, in too many cases, the very reason that disciple making has been deemphasized. We seek a straightforward process of disciple making that will be a tool to help correct this. To that end, there is no better model to examine than that of Jesus. Dunn notes that "...it is essential to scrutinize the records of the original discipleship of Jesus, to gain insight into the spirit and character of the discipleship, in order to get some kind of yardstick by which to measure one's own discipleship."[5] Good stewardship demands that we measure the fruit God bears in us. Dunn suggests three components of biblical measurement. First, Jesus called them to follow, then He taught them, and finally He appointed them as His messengers.[6] The objective was the advancement of the Kingdom as stated in Matthew 28:19.

For the disciples, once commissioned, disciple making becomes the imperative assignment of them as Jesus' core Twelve. Consider His teaching on fruit.

> And he told this parable: "A man had a fig tree planted in his
> vineyard, and he came seeking fruit on it and found none. And he
> said to the vinedresser, 'Look, for three years now I have come

---

[3] James D. G. Dunn, *Jesus' Call to Discipleship* (New York: Cambridge University Press, 1992), 2.

[4] Dunn, *Jesus' Call*, 2.

[5] Dunn, *Jesus' Call*, 3.

[6] It is helpful to note here that this call-train-appoint-go motif was the same for Paul as it was for The Twelve. To make this statement, it follows that the author holds to the Arabia hypothesis of Paul whereby he was taught personally by the resurrected Jesus after his calling on the road to Damascus.

seeking fruit on this fig tree, and I find none. Cut it down. Why should it use up the ground?' And he answered him, 'Sir, let it alone this year also, until I dig around it and put on manure. Then if it should bear fruit next year, well and good; but if not, you can cut it down.'"[7]

As we apply this teaching to disciple making, it is God's fruit that we seek. Next, we apply the story, as we have asserted, there is a lack of disciple making (tending of the garden) and therefore only few disciples (little fruit) thus, a change is in order. This change occurs when disciple making begins (cultivation is the challenging work of digging and fertilizing). But how?

Confusion about Modern Methods

Michael J. Wilkins, a prolific and recognized scholar on discipleship, laments the fact that there is a state of confusion regarding how congregations (and movements) engage in disciple making. After a survey of modern discipleship systems and movements, he concludes that: "No consensus reigns in understanding what Jesus was doing" or "in what we should be doing in making disciples."[8] This astute observation sheds light on the problem. There is vast array of sometimes competing styles of discipleship programs, books, and conferences available.

Programs?

Disciples are seldom the fruit of a system. Over time, in various contexts, I have seen leaders attend conferences and return with great enthusiasm about discipleship idea and programs. A pastor may learn that the congregation can grow in numbers and in depth with a discipleship system. The books and videos are ordered, the podcasts are listened to and interested members of the congregation gather for a weekend conference. The attendees are excited and get started, but in a couple of months, the enthusiasm is gone and things in the congregation are back to where they were at the beginning. The effect of the program lasted about as long as the banner introducing it.

---

[7] Luke 13:6-9.

[8] Michael Wilkins, *Following the Master: A Biblical Theology of Discipleship* (Grand Rapids, MI: Zondervan Publishing Co., 1992), Kindle ed., 11.

Wilkins provides an apt analysis. "Sometimes our discipleship programs thwart true discipleship. What I mean by this is that we can become so involved with our programs that we isolate ourselves from real life."[9] Wilkins's assertion is correct. Where does one go for direction? We assert that the Gospels are the place to go and the answer is surprisingly simple. But we must not confuse simple with easy. Coleman asserts that the answer from Jesus is a strategy of personal interaction. "The time which Jesus invested in these few disciples was so much more by comparison to that given to others that it can only be regarded as a deliberate strategy."[10] Jesus was deliberate in His investment in the Twelve. This approach should seem obvious, but the lack of its practice today reveals the opposite. If we are to engage disciples as Jesus did, we must dedicate time for deliberate and vulnerable honesty in face to face conversations. These collaborations should be with "persons to whom we open our lives"[11] and who therefore "see our many shortcomings. But let them also see a readiness to confess our sins when we understand the error of our ways."[12] It is in this kind of relationship that we can help one another understand and live the commands of Jesus.

Understanding Jesus' Method Dispels Confusion

Indeed, we assert that, biblically, fellow disciples walk together and focus on Jesus as their Master. Old Testament scholar Brad Young states. "The disciple walks with God by living out in practice the teaching of his rabbi."[13] As our Rabbi, we look to Jesus' as our model and for our imperative. To learn His teaching, an emphasis must be placed on reading Scripture together for understanding. In this way, we walk with Him in life just as did the Twelve.

In our exploration of Rabbinic Judaism in Chapter Five, Young suggests that there is a significant similarity between the rabbis of the Pharisee party and Jesus and His Twelve. He describes six similarities: 1) call, 2) conduct, 3) learning by observation, 4) working alongside their master as

---

[9] Wilkins, *Following the Master,* 8.

[10] Coleman, *Master Plan of Evangelism,* 41.

[11] Coleman, *Master Plan of Evangelism,* 78.

[12] Coleman, *Master Plan of Evangelism,* 78.

[13] Brad Young, *Meet the Rabbis: Rabbinic Thought and the Teachings of Jesus* (Peabody, MA: Hendrickson Publishers, 2007), 31.

apprentices, 5) being sent on assignment and reporting back, and 6) accountability to the Master's supervision.[14] This is a more comprehensive outline than that which Dunn provides. In its detail, Young's list is not just a checklist for measurement but an outline for studying the ministry of Jesus. In the 19th century A. B. Bruce wrote an extensive treatment of Jesus' method. Wilkins provides a helpful abstract of Bruce's nineteenth century classic, *The Training of the Twelve*[15], stating that he

> recognizes three stages in the history of the Twelve's relationship with Jesus. In the first stage they were simply believers in Jesus as the Christ and were his occasional companions (e.g., Jn 2:1, 12, 17, 22; 3:22; 4:1–27, 31, 43–45). In the second stage fellowship with Christ assumed the form of an uninterrupted attendance on his person, involving entire, or at least habitual abandonment of secular occupations (e.g., Mt 4:18–22; 9:9). In the third stage the twelve entered on the last and highest stage of their life's calling when they were chosen by the Master from the mass of his followers and formed into a select band to be trained for the great work of the apostleship.[16]

Bruce's model takes a different, might we say, natural, view of Jesus' disciple making. He begins by calling those who believed enough to follow, and selects and trains a few. It is wise to prayerfully seek those in whom to invest more deeply. From our larger circle of people, God will guide us to those with whom we enter a deeper spiritual formation.

---

[14] Cf. Young, *Meet the Rabbis*, 37 ff.

[15] A. B. Bruce, *The Training of the Twelve* (Grand Rapids, MI: Kregel Publishing Company, 1977), Kindle ed.

[16] Wilkins, *Following the Master*, 22.

Applicative Questions

What do you respond to the assertion that church attendance is a poor gauge for a healthy church?

What are the ways you could adapt Dunn's summation of Jesus' invite-teach-appoint model to disciple making in your context?

Who in your circle could you invite to join you in following Jesus?

CHAPTER FOUR

EXAMINING THE MODEL OF JESUS

Facets of Jesus' Method

Jesus developed His disciples as He traveled beside, lived among, and dialogued with them. In what follows, we will explore the ways Jesus trained His pupils. With that, we turn to the Gospels as our source, one can find no better handbook for disciple making. From the Gospels, a sketch of Jesus' method of disciple making will emerge.

Could any teaching be more important than the subject of prayer? Not only did the disciples hear Jesus teach about prayer, they saw Jesus' personal commitment to pray. *The Training of the Twelve*, A. B. Bruce purports that "a disciple, in all probability one of the Twelve, after hearing Jesus pray, made the request: 'Lord, teach us to pray, as John also taught his disciples.'"[1] The result, of course, was the Lord's Prayer which has become a model for millions during the two millennia since that request. For Luther,[2] this prayer would become an outline for one's daily prayer. Jesus was guiding their spiritual development through prayer which would become essential to strengthen them for the tests they would face. A critical emphasis in our disciple making conversations needs to be prayer.

Jesus taught by involving the Twelve in the act of serving others, not just telling them about it or telling them to serve. Bruce asserts that to observe and then actually be involved in the work of helping was more effective than simply hearing stories.[3] Today, this is called service-learning and in many places, is a device to develop volunteerism in contexts where such an

---

[1] A. B. Bruce, *The Training of the Twelve*, location 1091. We may also infer here that there was similar method to the disciple making of John the Baptist.

[2] Martin Luther, *A Simple Way to Pray*. Timothy Keller picks this up with the use of the Lord's Prayer as an outline for praying. We will look more deeply into this Part Three.

[3] Bruce, *Training of the Twelve*, location 971.

ethos has not developed. Service-learning is an effective disciple making method because of the collaborations and conversations that emerge while serving together. Consider the role of the Twelve at the feedings. They distributed, collected and then, upon inventorying the remainder, they reported to Jesus. But as significant as an act of service is, it is the motivation, the heart behind the act, that is imperative to mold. Jesus modeled compassion and this taught them what should be at the heart of the service. Jesus states: "I have compassion on the crowd,"[4] then He engaged them in serving. Serving, the visible evidence of being a disciple of Jesus should have proper motivation. This emerges in the heart that is being developed through prayer and Scripture reading, through personal discipleship and walking with fellow disciples. The lessons learned in action are moved from the head to the heart through discussions with the Master. But sometimes evaluation bears more fruit in a more private consultation after an event.

In the aftermath of His casting out the unclean spirit from a boy, as recorded in the Gospel of Mark, the disciples did not understand their ineffectiveness. A debriefing with the Master ensued behind closed doors. Mark records the event. "And when he had entered the house, his disciples asked him privately, 'Why could we not cast it out?' And he said to them, 'This kind cannot be driven out by anything but prayer.'"[5] Their failures were several-fold. Jesus used this conversation to teach them an important lesson on prayer. We may infer that it was a lesson of prayer over action. We must rely on God's power, not only over demons, but rather than our own works.

Indeed, some of the clearest teachings Jesus gave His pupils were the instructions recorded in Matthew 10. Jesus, like other rabbis of the time, would test His pupils. In this case, they would go, follow His commands, and report back to Him. Bruce details the Master's instructions prior to sending them out. He encouraged them to "have no fear..."[6] as they went. He spoke to them about their interactions with people, telling them to "...be wise as serpents and innocent as doves.[7] He warned them of the danger ahead. "Beware of men."[8] Jesus told them to have faith when authorities oppose them. "When they deliver you over, do not be anxious how you are to speak

---

[4] Mark 8:2.
[5] Mark 9:28-29.
[6] Matthew 10:26.
[7] Matthew 10:16.
[8] Matthew 10:17.

or what you are to say, for what you are to say will be given to you in that hour."[9] Bruce summarizes: "Such were the instructions of Christ to the Twelve when He sent them forth to preach and to heal."[10] They learned from His instructions, their participation and the debriefing.

As they lived and walked beside one another day by day, Jesus built upon their previous learning with more teachings. Much of that learning took place as they heard his teachings to the various crowds, both large and small, as well as among themselves. His teaching included confrontations. On the day following the feeding of the 5000, Jesus questioned the motives of a gathering of onlookers. On arrival at the shore of the lake, Jesus challenged them. "'Truly, truly, I say to you, you are seeking me, not because you saw signs, but because you ate your fill of the loaves.'"[11] He was aware of the motives of the people who had rushed around the lake seeking more spectacle. He was also teaching his disciples an important lesson about intent. A. B. Bruce pondered whether they loved Jesus for His own sake, or "only for the sake of expected worldly advantage."[12] This is an important question: Are the gathered crowds converts, disciples or just onlookers? Are they seeking God's kingdom or a free fellowship meal? The Lord, of course, knows the heart of each. This question goes right to the crux of our inquiry that differentiates between today's so-called 'cultural Christians',[13] seekers, and actual disciples of Jesus. This event should cause disciples everywhere to pause and examine their own hearts and minds. At this juncture, it is important to affirm the importance of teaching and preaching to groups, as in a local congregation. The difficulty, however, lies when attractive preaching is

---

[9] Matthew 10:19.

[10] Bruce, *Training of the Twelve*, location 2360.

[11] John 6:26.

[12] Bruce, *Training of the Twelve*, location 2534.

[13] This idea of so-called 'cultural Christians' described in Part Two is a challenge to the church in virtually every culture. Whether it be Hungarians who fit this because they depend on some dedication their grandparents made in the Lutheran church, Croat Catholics, Serb Orthodox or American 'Evangelicals.' The widespread idea that church attendance somehow gives me safety in heaven and favor here, and worse - prosperity, is perhaps one of the the biggest detriments to disciple making and therefore the strongest challenge to the Great Commission. When converts feel they pay their dues with a weekly trip to the warehouse of converts, they feel no need to be a disciple of Jesus and live in a kind of ignorant bliss.

not tied to disciple making. There needs to be something like what we referred to earlier, and now call the pulpit-table tandem. Preaching, that equips the disciple and is tied to disciple making, moves truth into the mind and heart and out into the world.

Not just the hearts of onlooking crowds, Bruce asserts, Jesus also challenges the motives of the Twelve "in the episode concerning Peter."[14] On the sea, Peter exclaims "...Lord, if it is you, command me to come to you on the water."[15] Bruce raises an apt concern as he restates the narrative. He states that

> ...on receiving permission, he [Peter] forthwith stepped out of the ship into the sea. This was not faith, but simple rashness. It was the rebound of an impetuous, headlong nature from one extreme of utter despair to the opposite extreme of extravagant, reckless joy. What in the other disciples took the tame form of a willingness to receive Jesus into the ship, after they were satisfied it was He who walked on the waters, took, in the case of Peter, the form of a romantic, adventurous wish to go out to Jesus where He was, to welcome Him back among them again. The proposal was altogether like the man — generous, enthusiastic, and well-meant, but inconsiderate.[16]

Bruce's analysis is that Peter's action is based on a complex personality that is characterized as "generous, enthusiastic, and well-meant, but inconsiderate."[17] Like Peter, we all struggle with complexities of personality, they need to be brought into the light of the gospel. This is what Jesus did in teachable moments with Peter and the other eleven. He used events as teachable moments to engage his pupils. With Bruce's analysis in mind, we need to be strategic. Our disciple making dialogues should bring our idiosyncrasies into the light of the gospel. Additionally, we should also recognize, from Peter's responses, that our expression of Christianity is not based solely on, to borrow from Bruce, romantic vision, personal enthusiasm, or experiences. Instead, disciple making should be biblically focused on Jesus.

A singular method of Jesus is His brilliant use of questions from which we may learn much. To that end, we turn to David Daube's discussion

---

[14] Bruce, *Training of the Twelve,* location 2689.
[15] Matthew 14:28.
[16] Bruce, *Training of the Twelve,* location 2689.
[17] Bruce, *Training of the Twelve,* location 2689.

of how "Socratic Interrogation"[18] was present in some of the interactions of Jesus. Daube referred to the form as "public retort-private explanation."[19] He explains that this form had four components. The elements are: "(1) hostile question by an outsider, (2) reply sufficient to defeat him, (3) request by the inner circle for the true reply and (4) the true reply."[20] To illustrate Daube's analysis, we examine the incident of the authority of Jesus' being challenged by the chief priests in the Temple. Let's look first at the text:

> By what authority are you doing these things, and who gave you this authority?" Jesus answered them, "I also will ask you one question, and if you tell me the answer, then I also will tell you by what authority I do these things. The baptism of John, from where did it come? From heaven or from man?" And they discussed it among themselves, saying, "If we say, 'From heaven,' he will say to us, 'Why then did you not believe him?' But if we say, 'From man,' we are afraid of the crowd, for they all hold that John was a prophet." So, they answered Jesus, "We do not know." And he said to them, "Neither will I tell you by what authority I do these things.[21]

This instance stands above other examples of its type in the Synoptics as the public retort model per Daube's analysis.

(1) "By what authority are you doing these things?" - Hostile question.
(2) "The baptism of John, from where did it come?" - Counter question.
(3) "We do not know," an admission that they dare not challenge the claims of the Baptist. This answer enables Jesus to proceed to

---

[18] Daube, David, *The New Testament and Rabbinic Judaism* (Peabody, MA: Hendrickson Publishers, 1956), 151. This will be considered in more detail in the next chapter.

[19] Daube, *New Testament*, 151.

[20] Daube, *New Testament*, 151. It should be clarified that there is a difference between Daube's outline and a strict interpretation of Socrates' method as presented in Chapter Six. As the Greek pedagogy migrated, adaptation and contextualization would certainly have taken place.

[21] Matthew 21:23-27.

(4) the rejoinder: "Neither will I tell you by what authority I do these things."[22]

Jesus was a master of the use of questions, counter-questions and answers. We must also note His brilliance in the use of the teachable moment. This stems from His genius at paying attention. This is a skill in which far too many teachers have a tragic deficiency.[23] His questions were designed to set context and tone, to challenge, motivate and prod minds for understanding, and to correct error.

Questions and Answers in Jesus' Method

To apply this approach to our own disciple making requires us to develop our listening skills and then recognize and use teachable moments where the question and answer method can bring understanding. According to research carried out for this project,[24] the use of the question and answer method by Jesus described above occurs fifteen times in the Synoptics. The investigation into the Synoptics reveals that there are seventy-one separate

---

[22] Daube, *New Testament,* 152. Daube's original outline of Matthew 21:23ff used the Authorized Version, we have substituted the English Standard Version and include more of the text for greater clarity.

[23] It is also worth mentioning that Daube points out how "The pattern accords with a Greek rhetorical rule." Daube, *New Testament,* 152. To be clear, it is not here asserted that Jesus followed these rules intentionally or even that he knew about them. It is asserted that these methods were already in play and used widely by rabbis by the time of His ministry. He did not have to follow the teaching method of the Greeks or anyone. He is, after all, the God who gave the Greeks the ability to do philosophy in the first place. It is without a doubt that because all those great minds mentioned had the image of God - indeed of this very Son of God, Jesus - that they could do this great reasoning. Thus, if these methods were widely used, it would make sense that he would use them.

[24] To further my understanding, a survey was made of the Synoptic Gospels in which all the questions Jesus asked were identified and categorized. Having catalogued all the questions, my objective was to determine how many questions he asked, the numerous ways he asked questions and how it is a means for us to ask good questions in disciple making. The results are found in Appendix A.

events (up to His crucifixion) in which Jesus uses questions.[25] When comparing event to event, the Synoptics record some 171 different questions that Jesus asks as He teaches and preaches.[26] In that considerable number we find the following breakdown. Four questions were a facet of a prophesy.[27] There were nineteen simple questions that were connected to some action or event, usually a miracle or as part of a narrative.[28] The second most frequent type of question are those which challenge His listeners, occurring twentieth-three times.[29] The largest category consists of questions that were directly connected to His teaching and the occurrence of teachable moments. This type includes the following: rhetorical questions, beginning a teaching with a question, a summary question at the end of a lesson, and occasions when he asked if his hearers understood. This includes the form analyzed above by Daube. Included are other instances where one can see Jesus ask a series of questions. This kind of interaction - usually two or three questions in rapid succession - guides His hearers to grasp His point. This is the clearest use of a 'Socratic Interrogation' form that will be explored in the next chapter. Along with parables and sermons, and included *in those* parables and sermons,

---

[25] Because of the nature of the Gospel narratives, I considered any change as a separate event. Only sections of the narrative that included questions, any questions, were included in the study. If the narrative shows a meaningful change of topic without indicating a change of location or hearers, the section was still counted separately. The purpose was to catch any nuance in His tone as a new subject may indicate.

[26] If a question is repeated in the same narrative in more than one Synoptic, all the Gospels that render that narrative were compared and the question was only counted once. This includes if a question a little differently is rendered a little differently from Mark to Matthew, that question is only counted once. The process was a bit like creating a harmony of the Gospels such as in A. T, Robertson, *A Harmony of the Gospels for Students of the Life of Christ* (New York, Harpers and Row Publishers, 1922). In this survey, a harmony of the questions emerged.

[27] "Do you see these great buildings? There will not be left here one stone upon another that will not be thrown down." Mark 13:2.

[28] "And he asked them, 'How many loaves do you have?' They said, 'Seven.'" Mark 8:5.

[29] "He said to them, 'Where is your faith?' And they were afraid, and they marveled, saying to one another, 'Who then is this, that he commands even winds and water, and they obey him?'" Luke 8:25.

questions were a primary method that Jesus used in developing the understanding of his pupils.

This is instructive and should be a part of our own disciple making process. Thus, in our conversations we should practice good listening, which is a result of paying careful attention. Comprehending the other person's words and context will enable us to ask questions that facilitate further understanding. Every person wishes to be heard, understood, and valued; this should be a basic function of disciple making, how else can we shine the gospel into lives? I contend that this is more readily accomplished across a lunch table than from a pulpit and is a skill that is learned through practice. Not the type of skill one can easily learn from a conference, it requires one to be attentive during regular heart-to-heart talks.

Paying Attention to One's Own Discipleship

One word of exhortation, caution even, practicing proper personal discipleship is, without a doubt, the essential first step. Unless leaders maintain their own proper focus on God and boundaries in life, there is no doubt that the demands of ministry will devour most of their time. The result is that leaders, marriages, families[30] and eventually the congregations themselves are neglected because busy schedules replace personal discipleship. A program can do little, if anything, about personal discipleship, but a disciple making relationship can. To our point about disciple making, we borrow from Charles Hummel[31] who asserts that the urgencies of ministry crowd out the importance of time with God. Wilkins considered several prominent disciple making strategies. Generally, we may infer from his

---

[30] In *Emotionally Healthy Spirituality*, Peter Scazerro discusses his own journey down this rabbit hole of overly busy ministry. He describes how his wife refused to attend the church he pastored due to the neglect she experienced. He then goes on to describe a way back *Emotionally Healthy Spirituality* (Grand Rapids, MI, Zondervan, 2006). In *Fail*, J. R. Briggs tells stories of leadership failures that should bring pause to leaders of all types of ministries. In each case, we assert, being in a disciple making relationship could have prevented such failure *Fail*, (Downer's Grove, IL., InterVarsity, 2014). Both of these works belong in the library of all leaders.

[31] Charles Hummel, *Tyranny of the Urgent* (Downer's Grove, IL., InterVarsity, 1967).

analysis that they fall short in one way or another.[32] Rather, let's remember our earlier application of Jesus' parable of the fig tree and "dig around it and put on manure. Then if it should bear fruit next year, well and good; but if not, you can cut it down."[33] Programs may show excellent short term instructional value, but have not consistently produced lasting fruit. Let's consider another way.

Friendship, Conversation, and Disciple Making

My own experience in disciple making is that God uses His disciples in regular conversation to strengthen one another. Simply put, the best ways for us to learn are through reading, studying and praying the Bible and asking one another questions about how those texts apply to life. We must not try to be disciples in isolation. Robert Meye, former Dean of Theology at Fuller Seminary, reminds us that in Jesus' context "the disciple did not exist in isolation."[34] Jesus' preaching drew crowds and from those crowds, He strategically chose disciples. These were present for, subject to, and the object of many of the questions He asked.

Disciples should bear fruit. Jesus challenges His disciples to that end. This requires one to move out in faith rather than being hampered by fear. "And he said to them, 'Why are you afraid, O you of little faith?' Then he rose and rebuked the winds and the sea, and there was a great calm."[35] The

---

[32] Wilkins examined major views on discipleship and shows the strengths and shortcomings of each. To repeat that here would not be a good use of space. While his analysis had a theological tilt that colors his conclusions, it is nonetheless an important piece of scholarship that provides a helpful review. It is, however, like all of the book, heavily weighted with American Evangelical sources. His work relies heavily on comparisons between Jesus and John the Baptist and their disciple making philosophies, the work of Josephus and regular consideration of the use of the word disciple in the book of Acts. I find none of these to be of great weight in the inquiry at present and will not mention them further. Wilkins is an important work in this area of study and his other insights will be helpful in other ways. Cf. Wilkins *Following the Master*, Ch. 2.

[33] Luke 13:6-9.

[34] Robert Meye, *Jesus and the Twelve: Discipleship and Revelation in Mark's Gospel* (Grand Rapids, MI: William B. Eerdmans Publishing Company, 1968), 32.

[35] Matthew 8:26.

God who rebukes the weather, and overcomes it, is our Master. How can we help fellow disciples in the areas of fear, faith and fruit? We aid one another through regular, vulnerable and honest conversations that point to the power and majesty of Jesus. We remind one another of His teachings on fear and anxiety. God can use us in these relationships to build one another's faith.

Jesus sought understanding. He would pause after a teaching, perhaps look around at the listeners, and ask: "'Have you understood all these things?' They said to him, 'Yes.'"[36] He demonstrates the characteristics of the master teacher when He insures his pupil's comprehension of the lessons. Too often we enjoy the sound of our own voices. A carefully posed question with an appropriate pause for thought can make the difference between our fellow-learner's understanding and their remaining in unawareness. Jesus paid attention to his learners. Listening and paying attention as modeled by Jesus are skills we should seek to develop.

Having examined the method of Jesus and the lessons we may learn from Him, we now examine the historical context in which His disciple making occurred. In the next chapter, we explore the rabbis who were making disciples around Jesus and then consider how the Socratic method of question and answer made its way into their first century BC Palestine context.

Applicative Questions

What significant lesson from our study of Jesus' method can you apply in your context this week?

Who are the people that would benefit from your improving your listening skills by paying attention?

What are examples of the teaching questions of Jesus that you can adapt for use in your disciple making conversations?

---

[36] Matthew 13:51.

CHAPTER FIVE

TORAH BASED DISCIPLE MAKING

From the model of Jesus, we may assert that questions and answers
are an important method in making disciples, particularly in conversations
that are pointed toward such. These conversations facilitate a richer
knowledge of God and deeper relationship with Him. Now we turn to
examine the historical context in which Jesus made disciples. To consider that
context, we examine a brief chronology of disciple making beginning with the
Old Testament, continue to the Greeks[1] and then to their pedagogical
influence on Rabbinic paradigms. The objective will be to further our
understanding of what a disciple is and how he or she was developed in the
time of Jesus. Looking first at Judaism, we ask: What is a disciple in the
context of the Old Testament?

Disciples in the Old Testament?

Were there disciples, such as we think of them now, in the Old
Testament? Let's begin with some etymology. Old Testament authority, Brad
Young states that "the Hebrew *talmid* is the equivalent of the Greek *mathētēs*."[2]
He adds that "Jerome translated *mathētēs* into Latin using *discipulus*. In Latin,
disco means 'to study', and from this root comes our English word 'disciple.'"[3]
Learning is essential to being a disciple, as well as the element of obedience.

---

[1] K. H. Rengstorf provides a helpful analysis of the variations in the
Greek philosophical schools in his discussion of 'disciple' in K. H. Rengstorf,
"*mathánō.*" in *Theological Dictionary of the New Testament*, ed. Gerhard Kittel and
Gerhard Friedrich, trans., abr. ed., ed., Geoffrey W. Bromiley (Grand Rapids:
Eerdmans Publishing, 1985), 552ff.

[2] Brad Young, *Meet the Rabbis: Rabbinic Thought and the Teachings of Jesus*
(Peabody, MA: Hendrickson Publishers, 2007), 30.

[3] Young, *Meet the Rabbis,* 30. This is especially intriguing in light of
our earlier consideration of Jerome's translation of *mathēteusate*. Indeed, this is
additional insight that this translation is part of the problem (stated earlier)
since we see that Jerome did use the word *discipulus* in other places.

Following this etymological introduction, Young elaborates.

> The Master-disciple model was extremely effective in late second temple and early rabbinic Judaism. The word for "disciple" in Hebrew is *talmid* (plural: *talmidim*). It really means "learner," one who is open to change and is actively seeking to learn how to live life to its fullest potential in the kingdom of heaven.[4]

Let's reconsider these two characteristics before moving further. First, a disciple should be "open to change."[5] We might say teachable, correctable or coachable. But isn't this willingness often dependent on one's growth in humility? It is difficult to learn when pride creates a roadblock. One may recall the stories of Augustine and Luther to see the importance of this characteristic. Augustine in the garden and Luther in the storm, both cried out in humility, from that, they became powerful tools of God in building His kingdom. One thinks of God's reply to Paul's struggle: "'My grace is sufficient for you, for my power is made perfect in weakness.'" To which Paul exclaims: "Therefore I will boast all the more gladly of my weaknesses, so that the power of Christ may rest upon me."[6] It is through humility that we learn. Secondly, the disciple must be "seeking to learn how to live life to its fullest potential in the kingdom of heaven."[7] As the Pietist Jacob Spener[8] emphasized, that we learn not just the Bible, but we apply biblical teaching to life and then do as we have learned. Having considered a brief introduction to different forms of the word disciple, we now turn to historical context. Initially, a look at the Old Testament is in order followed by an examination of the Hellenistic influence on first century B.C. Rabbinic Judaism.

The Old Testament does not describe or give direct examples of the kind of disciple making seen in Jesus' work. There are however several instances that have application to our inquiry. Wilkins asserts that the "roots of biblical discipleship go deep into the fertile soil of God's calling."[9] He

---

4 Young, *Meet the Rabbis*, 32.

5 Young, *Meet the Rabbis*, 32.

6 2 Corinthians 12:9.

7 Young, *Meet the Rabbis*, 30.

8 We will explore the influence of Spener in Part Three.

9 Michael Wilkins, *Following the Master: A Biblical Theology of Discipleship* (Grand Rapids, MI: Zondervan Publishing Co., 1992), Kindle ed., 39.

explains that this interaction of call and response is "the biblical concept of covenant."[10] To give examples of these Old Testament relationships, he reminds the reader that "Joshua and Elisha are designated by God to carry out the work of their masters, Moses and Elijah."[11] God designated these men to follow two great Hebrew figures. But it was God Himself who directed them. To illustrate, consider God's meeting with Moses in The Tabernacle. "And you shall put it [the altar] in front of the veil that is above the ark of the testimony, in front of the mercy seat that is above the testimony, *where I will meet with you* [emphasis mine]."[12] God chose Moses to speak through and lead the people. Moses had direct conversations with God who later speaks to his people through other chosen prophets and kings. We may glean from these examples that it is God's plan that He be our Master. This correlates with our understanding of Jesus as our Master today. But, does this constitute the kind of disciple making we see Jesus practicing? It does not. The difference is the Incarnation. Perhaps it is helpful at this juncture to go back to the primordial human relationship with God.

Relationship with God: Established, Broken, Suspended

Consider the Garden where God and man walked together and God provided for man. Humans were made in the image of God. The very nature of the Trinity is community: Father Son and Spirit. Thus, we are not designed to live in isolation.[13] "the LORD God said, 'It is not good that man should be alone;'"[14] then He creates Eve. This is a glimpse of community between God and His two image-bearers. We see communication and collaboration between God and Adam (the naming of the animals in Genesis 2:19-20).

---

[10] Wilkins, *Following the Master*, 39.

[11] Wilkins, *Following the Master*, 49.

[12] Exodus 30:6.

[13] The disciple does not thrive in isolation. Meye asserts that primary attention be devoted to Jesus (as Lord and teacher) as the key to the meaning of discipleship. Being with Jesus being His pupil in relationship is the key. This can be better understood if the term "learner" is substituted for the word 'disciple'." Robert Meye, *Jesus and the Twelve: Discipleship and Revelation in Mark's Gospel* (Grand Rapids, MI: William B. Eerdmans Publishing Company, 1968), 32. The 'isolation' Meye mentions is important. Jesus made disciples though human on human contact.

[14] Genesis 2:18.

Adam and Eve interact directly with God in the garden as was God's plan and wish. Further, in Genesis 3:8 we see "God walking in the garden…"[15] But, the nature of that interaction was suspended in His just response to The Fall. Because of sin, they are cast from Eden as the relationship has changed, for them and for us all, their progeny. Then, God promises that a redeemer will come.

Throughout the amazing story of the Old Testament, God cared for, taught and guided the people of Israel. Yet, there was a separation that could not be overcome until the Incarnation and the finished work of Christ. Now, as disciples of Jesus, walking with God is possible again. This is the renewal of relationship between the personal God of the Trinity and His image bearing creation through discipleship with Jesus as our Master. The Incarnation is key to fulfilling what the Old Testament can only promise. Wilkins explains that "…the relationship established between God and Israel was a divine-human relationship that anticipated the relationship to which Jesus would call his followers."[16] Christ's first advent provided the opportunity for relationship with God again. We see this through His disciple making.

Relationship with God: Restored

Jesus shared meals, journeyed beside and worshiped in synagogues with His disciples. This is different from the God to human model we see in the Old Testament. Today, in obedience to the Great Commission, we can make disciples *as we go forth* because He sent the Holy Spirit to us. We become disciple making agents of Jesus, walking in collaboration, not giving dictate to fellow disciples. Rather, *we point one another to Him.*

Personal relationships in the Hebrew Scriptures, therefore, look toward Christ. "The Old Testament theme of God with his people," Wilkins declares, "finds explicit fulfillment in Jesus with his people."[17] Asserting that the Old Testament prepared us, Wilkins qualifies those assertions: "We should not press too far in the direction of drawing unwarranted analogous continuity between what we see in the Old Testament and the New Testament, nor too far in the direction of claiming unwarranted

---

[15] Genesis 3:8.

[16] Wilkins, *Following the Master*, 53.

[17] Wilkins, *Following the Master*, 52.

discontinuity.[18] Therefore, we examine the Old Testament for context more than for example. Wilkins cautions against discounting the Old Testament. He states that even though there is "a curious scarcity of Hebrew and Aramaic words for 'disciple,'" we should be careful not to "minimize discipleship concepts in the Old Testament."[19] We consider the Hebrew Scriptures with gratitude to God for relationship models therein, but by the time we get to Jesus, the model has changed. No longer does God rule through kings or speak through prophets, for He has come among us, Emmanuel.

The Place of the Old Testament in Disciple Making of Rabbinic Judaism

The Law and the Prophets are essential to Jesus' disciple making method as well as to those of His contemporaries, rabbis of the Hillel school of Rabbinic Judaism. The Torah was the core curriculum of teachers of Rabbinic Judaism in the time surrounding the Incarnation. Jesus knew this well. When a Pharisee asks about divorce, His reply was "What did Moses command you?"[20] With a similar emphasis, as He told the story of Lazarus and the rich man, Jesus emphasizes the importance of hearing "Moses and the Prophets."[21] In the teaching of Jesus and the Apostles it is clear the Old Testament was and remains pertinent. As we examine the method of the rabbis it is evident that Scripture (at that time only the Hebrew Bible) is imperative.

---

[18] Wilkins, *Following the Master*, 40.

[19] Wilkins, *Following the Master*, 42.

[20] Mark 10:3.

[21] "'Then I beg you, father, to send him to my father's house—for I have five brothers—so that he may warn them, lest they also come into this place of torment.' But Abraham said, 'They have Moses and the Prophets; let them hear them.' And he said, 'No, father Abraham, but if someone goes to them from the dead, they will repent.' He said to him, 'If they do not hear Moses and the Prophets, neither will they be convinced if someone should rise from the dead.'" (Luke 16:27-31).

The Torah: Foundation of Disciple Making?

Exhaustive learning and application of the Torah[1] was essential to first century B.C. Judaism. From the Exile to Babylon in the 6th century B.C. with its cessation of temple worship and the development of the Synagogues, many rabbis would have the Torah memorized. It is implausible to think that every Synagogue that grew up in the period of exile would have an exhaustive supply of the Law. Thus, the memorization of the Scriptures became paramount to Jews, especially the rabbis and elders. Paraphrases, *Targumim,* were developed and widely used during the captivity. Under Ezra, the Scribes first developed as copiers and then interpreters of the Torah. Eventually, there would be an expectation that the entire Torah was, literally, in mind. Saul Lieberman, former Professor of Talmud at the Jewish Theological Seminary of America, asserts that "there is no evidence that the rabbis prepared special lexica of the Bible; they had no need for them. The entire rabbinic literature bears testimony to the fact that the Rabbis knew the Bible by heart."[2] To these Jewish teachers, the Law was their primary focus in all matters theological and practical.[3] It is important here to note that Jesus was

---

[1] The first five books of the Old Testament.

[2] Saul Lieberman, *Hellenism in Jewish Palestine* (New York: Jewish Theological Seminary, 1962), 52.

[3] It goes without saying that the Scribes and Pharisees had added much to the Law. Jesus condemned such. "Now when the Pharisees gathered to him, with some of the scribes who had come from Jerusalem, they saw that some of his disciples ate with hands that were defiled, that is, unwashed. (For the Pharisees and all the Jews do not eat unless they wash their hands properly, holding to the tradition of the elders, and when they come from the marketplace, they do not eat unless they wash. And there are many other traditions that they observe, such as the washing of cups and pots and copper vessels and dining couches.) And the Pharisees and the scribes asked him, "Why do your disciples not walk according to the tradition of the elders, but eat with defiled hands?" And he said to them, "Well did Isaiah prophesy of you hypocrites, as it is written,

"'This people honors me with their lips,
        but their heart is far from me;
    in vain do they worship me,
        teaching as doctrines the commandments of men.'

You leave the commandment of God and hold to the tradition of men." And

clear that he did not come to abolish, but to fulfil the Law.[4] The Scripture was the heart and soul of Judaism as they returned to Palestine to rebuild Jerusalem.

Torah Study Should Change Lives

Before they began studying under their master teachers, disciples of Jewish rabbis had memorized The Torah and were expected to bear the fruit of a changed life. "Torah learning is evidenced in behavior and a rich spiritual life." Young explains. "The *disciple walks with God* [emphasis mine] by living out in practice the teaching of his rabbi."[5] Likewise, our great rabbi, Jesus, is interested in fruit.

> Beware of false prophets, who come to you in sheep's clothing but inwardly are ravenous wolves. You will recognize them by their fruits. Are grapes gathered from thornbushes, or figs from thistles? So, every healthy tree bears good fruit, but the diseased tree bears bad fruit. A healthy tree cannot bear bad fruit, nor can a diseased tree bear good fruit. Every tree that does not bear good fruit is cut down and thrown into the fire. Thus you will recognize them by their fruits.[6]

This fruit is what Jesus required of His disciples, changed lives that follow His commands. Jacob Neusner, a leading authority on Rabbinic Judaism, describes the emphasis of bearing fruit. Rabbis insisted that the study of Scripture would change one's life in such a way that al who saw him would know him to be a disciple."[7] One can see a parallel emphasis in the disciple making words of Paul as he writes to his protégé, Timothy stating that the

---

he said to them, "You have a fine way of rejecting the commandment of God in order to establish your tradition!" Mark 7:1-9.

[4] "Do not think that I have come to abolish the Law or the Prophets; I have not come to abolish them but to fulfill them. For truly, I say to you, until heaven and earth pass away, not an iota, not a dot, will pass from the Law until all is accomplished." Matthew 5:17-18.

[5] Young, *Meet the Rabbis*, 31.

[6] Matthew 7:15-20.

[7] Jacob Neusner, *There We Sat Down: Talmudic Judaism in the Making* (Nashville, TN: Abingdon Press, 1971), 92.

Scripture is "profitable for teaching, for reproof, for correction, and for training in righteousness, that the man of God may be competent, equipped or every good work.[8] The 'Scripture' Paul refers to here, of course, is the Hebrew Bible. A careful reading of Paul shows his training in Rabbinic Judaism and in its disciple making methods. Before becoming a disciple of the Risen One, Paul was a disciple of Gamaliel. In each case the life of a disciple should be changed. The object is fruit of disciple making, not a works righteousness. With the Word of God ingrained in us, as we follow our Master, He changes us. These good works are fruit of our discipleship with Jesus, not vise-versa.

Pedagogy of Rabbinic Judaism

The Law was the basis of disciple making among the rabbis. But to further understand the context of Jesus as disciple maker, we look to the Gospels and to the methods of the rabbis of the time. Neusner gives an insightful introduction to how rabbinical schools functioned. The master instructed the disciples in the "traditions of the Torah. These were encapsulated in formulas, and the student memorized the exact words, not merely the sense, of those traditions."[9] Next the leader of the school was "a community authority, a judge, and administrator, so the disciple would follow the master as he did his business, keeping in mind the ways in which the master applied the law in specific cases."[10] We may surmise that Jesus' disciples also learned his teachings carefully. Likewise, they understood His example and commands and went forth to proclaim these teachings as He instructed in Matthew 10. All the lessons the Twelve learned as they studied under Jesus were imprinted in their minds and hearts. Years later, they penned or collaborated with other apostles as the Holy Spirit inspired them to produce the Gospels and the Epistles. Thus, we may consider our New Testament as a fruit of the disciple making of Jesus. Again, one should recall that Jesus did not come to put the Law aside, but to fulfill it.[11] His teaching was clear: at the heart of the Torah was the Shema. Jesus calls it the 'greatest

---

[8] 2 Timothy 3:16-17.

[9] Jacob Neusner, *There We Sat Down.* 96.

[10] Jacob Neusner, *There We Sat Down.* 96.

[11] It is helpful here to be reminded that Paul's admonition to Timothy cited above refers to the Old Testament.

commandment,' to which He adds another commandment to His hearers, to love their neighbor.[12] As a rabbi, Jesus never lost sight of the Mosaic Law. When compared to the methods of the other rabbis of the time, Jesus is not markedly different. This is a helpful understanding of the process. One that all disciple makers would do well to adapt into their context. Indeed, all these questions, answers, teachings and experiences developed the learners through training hearts and minds through what we might call mentoring.

Many experts use the ideas of mentoring, coaching, and apprenticeship to describe this process of disciple making. Young states that Jesus "developed a mentoring relationship with his disciples, who may have memorized his teachings and followed his example as apprentices. Jesus' teaching techniques have deep roots in the rich soils of Jewish education and Torah training."[13] Coaching, mentoring and consulting are widespread in western Christianity today. Are these the same as disciple making? Perhaps. But is that coaching, mentoring and consulting for spiritual development pointing disciples to Jesus, their true master? One of our Lord's objectives was to prepare His disciples for their part in building His kingdom. They too, in obedience to the Great Commission, would become disciple makers.

Obedience and Fruit in the Life of a Disciple

The purpose of discipleship by a rabbi was to live a life molded by the Torah and become a disciple-maker. Neusner asserts that a primary objective of being the disciple of a rabbi was to *become a rabbi* through discipleship.[14] A. B. Bruce describes it this way:

"Follow Me," said Jesus to the fishermen of Bethsaida, "and I will make you fishers of men." These words (whose originality stamps them as a genuine saying of Jesus) show that the great Founder of the faith desired not only to have disciples, but to have about Him men whom He might train to make disciples of others:[15]

---

[12] Cf. Mark 12:28ff.

[13] Young, *Meet the Rabbis*, 29.

[14] Neusner, *There We Sat Down.* 96.

[15] A. B. Bruce, *The Training of the Twelve* (Grand Rapids, MI: Kregel Publishing Company, 1977), Kindle ed., location 316.

Fruit bearing disciple making is the heart of this inquiry. One of the similarities between Jesus and the other rabbis is that they affect change in lives. They shared not only objectives but methods, especially that of teaching through dialogue facilitated by questions and answers. These intentional questions and answers are designed to bring learners to a point of understanding. Educators call this the Socratic method. This is especially true in the manner that Jesus used questions. We can see, in both the rabbis' and Jesus' methods the importance of questions. It was widely used decades before the Incarnation. We turn our attention to Athens to consider how this question and answer method was developed.

Applicative Questions

What are memorable experiences in your life in which a well posed question has made you think, and perhaps changed your mind on a matter? Or caused you to reflect more deeply about an issue in your own personal discipleship?

In your evangelism and apologetic endeavors, what are the ways that asking questions might cause people to think about the gospel instead of reacting to what they *think* you are doing?

In your evangelism and apologetic endeavors, are you seeking converts or disciples?

CHAPTER SIX

SOCRATIC INFLUENCE
ON DISCIPLE MAKING IN PALESTINE

Considering Greek Pedagogical Influence

About the time that Nehemiah was leading the Jews to complete the walls of Jerusalem following their return from exile, just 778 miles to the northwest in Athens, Socrates (469-300 B.C.)[1] was using his *elenchus*[2] in philosophical conversation. Socrates 'elenchus' was his method of logical refutation using questions and answers. He was using this in the context of, as scholar Gregory Vlastos describes, seeking moral truth.

> Socratic elenchus is a search for moral truth by question-and-answer adversary argument in which a thesis is debated only if asserted as the answerer's own belief and is regarded as refuted only if its negation is deduced from his own beliefs.[3]

Simply put, a question forces the answerer to consider his own idea again and respond to the question. That answer is then the basis of the next question, eliciting another answer. The objective of the questioner is to help his fellow conversationalist arrive at the truth of the matter. Vlastos looks to Plato's *Apology*, asserting that "Socrates' 'search' is, at the same time, a challenge to his fellows to change their lives, to cease caring for money and reputation and

---

[1] Debra Nails, s.v. "Socrates", *The Stanford Encyclopedia of Philosophy*, ed. Edward N. Zalta, http://plato.stanford.edu/archives/spr2014/entries/socrates/ (accessed 28 July 2016).

[2] The Socratic method is a process of teaching through careful questioning, leading to the student's understanding.

[3] Gregory Vlastos, "The Socratic Elenchus: Method is All" in *Socratic Studies*, ed. Myles Burnyeat (New York: Cambridge University Press, 1994), 4.

not caring for the most precious thing of all - what one is:"[4] Thus, there is a life change sought by Socrates in this inquiry to moral truth.

Active Learning

To understand the method as it is applied directly to a pedagogical context, we look to educator Alan Scott. He asserts that Socrates "forces his conversation partner to think and express his own thoughts prior to hearing what the much more thoughtful and experienced philosopher has to say on the subject. In this way, Socratic questioning promotes what some today called *active learning*."[5] Active learning, as opposed to the passive learning that one may find in a lecture or listening to a sermon is what fosters fellow disciple making. Again, we are to use the Scripture and help one another gain a growing understanding of, and live what God's Word proclaims. We are to help one another birth understanding and life application from the text of Scripture. This too has a direct parallel in Socrates and his method. "Socrates regarded himself as a midwife (*maieutria*) using this method to assist in the birth of ideas…"[6] Hence, as we examine and consider what the rabbis of the Hillel school were practicing, we may see this maieutic method at work. This method of inquiry is an important key to our current investigation to Rabbinic Judaism and the time of Jesus.

Jesus and Greek Rhetoric?

In his chapter "Socratic Interrogation" David Daube, preeminent scholar of ancient law, proposed that Jesus taught through questions and

---

[4] Vlastos, "Socratic Elenchus," 9.

[5] Alan Scott, *Plato's Socrates as Educator* (Albany, NY: State University Press, 2000), 45. Of further help, though very technical, is a treatment of Socrates himself and his use of the interrogation method in Hugh H. Benson "Socratic Method" In *Cambridge Companion to Socrates* (Cambridge, GB: Cambridge University Press, March 2011), 179-200, http://dx.doi.org/10.1017/CCOL9780521833424.008 (accessed 7/26/2016).

[6] Peter A. Angeles, s.v. "Socratic Method," *HarperCollins Dictionary of Philosophy*, 2nd ed., ed. Eugene Ehrlich (New York: HarperCollins, 1992), 282. Angeles completes the quote with the full idea of Socrates' epistemology (: morality) by saying "-ideas already formed and carried (impregnated) in the mind and the nature of human beings."

answers, His objective is understanding. This method mirrored those of Rabbinic Judaism which had, before Jesus time, absorbed the practice from the Greek pedagogy just described. In his discussion of Jesus' healing of a sick man on the Sabbath in Luke, Daube asserts that the method of Jesus "accords with a Greek rhetorical rule."[7] Further, "...it is plain that in the last few centuries B.C., the Rabbis drew on Hellenistic rhetoric in many fields."[8] This method had spread across cultures from Athens to the centers of culture and education: Rome, Alexandria, Tarsus, Jerusalem and others. Daube asserts that the widespread nature of the phenomenon was not a natural development. Instead, "...the form is not so natural that it would be handled by anybody and anywhere - it does not occur in the Old Testament...."[9] Questions and answers may not be considered a natural method of disseminating information because it is easier to stand before a classroom (or congregation) and impart information through lecture (or sermon) than to engage students with questions and answers and see understanding emerge.

How Might the Question and Answer Model Arrive in Palestine?

The fact that this question asking method was absent in the Old Testament but present among the rabbis by the time of Jesus in Palestine is significant. This form of education would have crossed cultures as educated migrants traveled throughout the Roman Empire. Consider that Synagogues developed around the Mediterranean as the Jewish diaspora continued their migration, as they had for over 500 years since the exile. Rabbis are needed to teach the Torah in Jewish communities in places like Thessalonica, Corinth, Athens, Ephesus, Rome and beyond. Distant synagogues would welcome traveling rabbis to teach the Torah. Pax Romana had made travel relatively safe. Roman roads had made travel viable. One need not be a historian to understand that, as time went by, these rabbis engaged with the cultures they lived in or to which they traveled. As such, a rabbi would have learned not just about the Hellenistic milieu in which he lived, but also about new methods of learning. When our hypothetical teacher returned to Palestine for Passover or Pentecost or other festivals, a collaboration and sharing of ideas

---

[7] David Daube, *The New Testament and Rabbinic Judaism* (Peabody, MA: Hendrickson Publishers, 1956), 152.

[8] Daube, *The New Testament*, 152.

[9] Daube, *The New Testament*, 155.

with colleagues would occur.[10] Indeed we may see the era as one of a crossing cultures and spreading ideas. What educators call the Socratic method, David Daube notes, "recurs in Cicero, Hillel and Plato - with enormous differences in detail, yet *au fond* the same."[11] He adds that "Cicero did not sit at the feet of Hillel, nor Hillel at the feet of Cicero."[12] While there may not have been direct connection, a more natural migration and adaptation of ideas would have occurred. There was significant exchange of scholarship between Jerusalem and Alexandria. To explore how this migration of ideas and teaching methods worked, we need simply consider the example of the Septuagint[13] which is, certainly, the most well-known fruit of the interaction. It was through this interaction that the Old Testament was translated into the vernacular of the Greek speaking Jews of Alexandria and beyond. Cross-cultural religious and academic exchange was alive and well by the time of the coming of Jesus.

Historical Context: Hillel, Gamaliel and Saul of Tarsus

The leader of Rabbinic Judaism before the birth of Christ was Hillel (circa. 110-10 BC). His direct influence was circa 30 BC to AD 10. He was by no means a stranger to cross-cultural exchange. Not a Palestinian Jew by birth, he spent the first third of his life in Babylon prior to his move to Palestine[14] by 30 BC.[15] He founded a school of thought in Rabbinic Judaism which took his name and emerged as dominant among Pharisees by the time of Jesus and continued well beyond. It was the school of Hillel in which Gamaliel was a foremost leader at the time of Jesus' ministry.

---

[10] Edersheim is helpful here. Alfred Edersheim, *The Life and Times of Jesus the Messiah* (Grand Rapid, MI, Wm. B. Eerdmans Publishing Co., 1971), 19ff.

[11] David Daube, *Rabbinic Methods* of Interpretation and Hellenistic Rhetoric" in *Hebrew Union College Annual*, Vol. XXII (Cincinnati, Ohio, Hebrew Union College, 949; repr. New York: KTAV Publishing, 1968), 257.

[12] Daube, *The New Testament*, 257.

[13] Second century BC Greek translation of Hebrew Scriptures performed in Alexandria, cf. de Hamel *The Book*, 46-47.

[14] Edersheim, *The Life and Times*, 128.

[15] Neusner was particularly helpful in the context of this study. Cf Jacob Neusner, "The Figure of Hillel" in *Judaism in the Beginning of Christianity* (Philadelphia, PA: Fortress Press, 1984), 63 ff.

This was the same Gamaliel who spoke up in response to the charges against Peter and John before the Sanhedrin in Acts. In that interaction, one can see the question and answer method at work in the way he reasoned with his colleagues. Using it, he won the release of Peter and John.[16] But the connection does not end here. We may rightly suppose that one of Gamaliel's finest pupils, Saul of Tarsus, was present and taking in this remarkable scene. This disciple of Gamaliel was soon called by and become a disciple of the risen Jesus. While its influence on the context is indisputable, we must not make too much of the Hillel school. As we study the method of Jesus in our quest for disciple making, we will see this question and answer method at work. We will delve deeper into our Master's method in the next chapter. Hillel's experience in crossing cultures would have made him interested in and open to ideas that originated elsewhere, whether Jerusalem, Alexandria or Athens. Daube notes that "...Hillel's ideas were partly imported from Egypt."[17] But, we must not, as Daube cautions, take this line of reasoning too far.

> In contending that this form comes from Hellenistic rhetoric, we do not claim that a New Testament narrative told in it goes back to a Hellenistic rather than a Jewish milieu. In that period, much of *Hellenistic rhetoric was the common property of the civilized Mediterranean world.*

---

[16] "When they heard this, they were enraged and wanted to kill them. But a Pharisee in the council named Gamaliel, a teacher of the law held in honor by all the people, stood up and gave orders to put the men outside for a little while. And he said to them, "Men of Israel, take care what you are about to do with these men. For before these days Theudas rose up, claiming to be somebody, and a number of men, about four hundred, joined him. He was killed, and all who followed him were dispersed and came to nothing. After him Judas the Galilean rose up in the days of the census and drew away some of the people after him. He too perished, and all who followed him were scattered. So in the present case I tell you, keep away from these men and let them alone, for if this plan or this undertaking is of man, it will fail; but if it is of God, you will not be able to overthrow them. You might even be found opposing God!" So they took his advice, and when they had called in the apostles, they beat them and charged them not to speak in the name of Jesus, and let them go." Acts 5:33-40.

[17] Daube, *New Testament*, 156-7.

[emphasis mine] Its effects are hardly less noticeable in Rabbinic literature than in Greek or Roman.[18]

Thus, the natural progression of this pedagogy migrated across Mediterranean civilization over the several centuries prior to the Incarnation.

From Hillel's School Emerges a Sharp Instrument of God

A specific example that is helpful at this point our inquiry is Saul of Tarsus. He would become the Apostle to the Gentiles and is an example of how this migration across cultures may have fostered such pedagogical exchange. Saul clearly had a command of Hellenistic culture. He demonstrated this understanding as he engaged the philosophers at Mars Hill, various Roman authorities, and Jewish royalty, among others. This understanding would have been acquired through his upbringing in Tarsus. Tarsus was a cosmopolitan city near an important seaport, on a trade route and itself a seat of education.[19] Eminent New Testament scholar F. F. Bruce describes it as "...what we might call a university city."[20] Benedict XVI notes: "Paul thus appears to be at the intersection between three different cultures - Roman, Greek and Jewish - and perhaps partly because of this was disposed for fruitful universalistic openness, for a mediation between cultures."[21] This intertwining of cultures and learning would explain how Paul's' writings would exhibit, as asserted by theology professor David Smith, "a flavour especially of the Stoic philosophy."[22] After his youth in Tarsus, young Saul studied under Gamaliel in the school of Hillel in Jerusalem. There may be no better example of a life developed in a cultural melting pot, in the time of Jesus, than Saul of Tarsus. This astounding timing, for Jesus to come at this great crossroads of history, facilitated by peace, at the hand of Rome, influenced by the civilization and learning of the teachers from Athens shows

---

[18] Daube, *New Testament*, 156-7.

[19] For an excellent introduction to Tarsus, cf. David Smith, *The Life and Letters of St. Paul* (New York: G. H. Doran, 1923), 17ff.

[20] F. F. Bruce, *Apostle of the Heart Set Free* (Grand Rapids, MI: William B. Eerdmans, 1977), 35, cf. 32ff.

[21] Benedict XVI, *Paul of Tarsus* (London, England: The Incorporated Catholic Truth Society, 2009), 15.

[22] Smith, *The Life and Letters of St. Paul* (New York: G. H. Doran Co., 1923), 24.

the great plan of God at work. This was a fitting time for the Incarnation, indeed, it was the apex of history.

All this asserts that there had been a natural spread of the question and answer dialogue method across cultures. The method had made its way into the master-disciple pedagogy in Palestine by the time of Jesus. That which we call the Socratic method, whether through formal instruction or natural discourse, had become part of the disciple making methodology by the first century AD. This use of questions, from Jesus forward, opens doors for cross-cultural dialogue and disciple making.

Method, Not Content

However, we do not imply that any form of syncretism existed between Rabbinic Judaism and the philosophy of the Greeks.[23] The point we investigate at this stage is a method of teaching, not the material taught. The reader should not infer that we adhere to or purport some Neoplatonic dualism, Aristotelian materialism, or anything else for that matter. We assert only that the question-answer teaching system made its way to Palestine and was being used profitably in disciple making by rabbis including Jesus.

The ramifications of this for *missio Dei* are significant. Jesus used a method that had already crossed cultures from Athens to Jerusalem and would continue to cross cultures from Asia to Africa to Europe. He modeled disciple making through dialogue. A dialogue that can be duplicated as one goes forward in mission. But, as Daube warned, we should not make too much of this. Making the disciple making method of Jesus into that of the Greek philosopher or of the Rabbi is reaching too far, they were only men, and for that matter, men with incomplete works righteousness theologies at that. Yet, there is little doubt, as one reads the Gospels, that the question and answer method was widely used by Jesus.

Daube provides insight into how Jesus used this method. His example is the occasion of Jesus being challenged about healing on the Sabbath. When challenged, Jesus answered with a series of questions. "Which one of you who has a sheep, if it falls into a pit on the Sabbath, will not take hold of it and lift it out? Of how much more value is a man than a sheep! So,

---

[23] Saul Lieberman discusses the ban of some Hellenist thought in "The Alleged Ban on Greek Wisdom" in Saul Lieberman, *Hellenism in Jewish Palestine* (New York: Jewish Theological Seminary, 1962). 100-114.

it is lawful to do good on the Sabbath."[24] Daube noted that these are "...applications of Hillel's first rule of exegesis."[25] It is our assertion that we as disciple-makers have much to learn from Jesus' question and answer technique. To be sure, we have much to learn from the questions themselves, perhaps beginning with one of the most important: "Who do you say that I am?"[26] This is a question that many who sit in church buildings on a given Sunday should ponder, but, sadly due to, perhaps a lack of curiosity, they do not. They are content to listen passively and not learn actively. If they do not struggle with this question, they may never be fruitful disciples. This is the tragedy that has spurred this project. If Wilkins is right, suggesting that "we may define a disciple as a committed follower of a great master,"[27] then there must be a renewal of commitment. A disciple must have a commitment to follow Jesus.

Having considered a biblical understanding of disciple making, examined the methods of Jesus and His context, we now consider the question, why did the making of disciples appear to fade from emphasis historically? This aspect of our inquiry will begin by following the hypothesis of Dietrich Bonhoeffer who asserts that a 'secularization' of the church is largely to blame. Our next step is a further exploration of Christian history on this subject.

Applicative Questions

As you considered the influence of Athens upon Judea, how did you respond?

Is it a challenge for you to consider that the methods of Jesus were much like those of the school of Hillel?

How could thoughtful questions help you in your teaching and disciple making? How could questions help your hearers understand your teaching in a deeper fashion?

---

[24] Matthew 12:11-12.

[25] Daube, *Rabbinic Methods*, 255-256.

[26] Mark 8:29.

[27] Wilkins, *Following the Master*, 26.

PART TWO:

EXPLORING

DISCIPLE MAKING

THROUGH HISTORY

CHAPTER SEVEN

RESPONDING TO CULTURAL CHRISTIANITY

Evangelism is critical to the Great Commission. Yet, it is only the first step on the lifelong journey of following Jesus as a disciple. We have asserted that investing in one another's growth throughout a life of following Jesus is the complete fulfillment of the Great Commission in Matthew 28:19. This is what we call disciple making. Having established an initial biblical understanding of disciple making in Chapter Two and then the methods and context of Jesus, we now consider the question, why did making disciples fade from emphasis historically? To that end, we explore some of the history of Christianity from the post-apostolic era forward. Our objective is to glean lessons from some of those who have gone before us. We will then apply what we have learned to disciple making.

To be Persecuted is a Mark of Being a Disciple

There was at its beginning of the Church a deep commitment to being a disciple (pupil, student of Jesus) and to making disciples. There is no greater proof of that commitment than the martyrs. During the first three Christian centuries, to be a disciple of Christ was often marked by severe, often fatal persecution. This persecution occurred during the first decades. The Way, as followers of Jesus were first known, was opposed by many Jews as seen in Acts. Following the expansion of the Church, the Roman government practiced persecution more broadly. Early disciples were charged with atheism because they refused to worship the emperor as lord. The Romans were a pluralistic culture but required adherents to other religions to affirm allegiance to Caesar as lord. This charge was leveled against many in the young Church under various regimes beginning with Nero and continuing until Constantine. In recurring waves of persecution from the first apostles through the early 4th century many met their death for Christ. To die for Jesus was the ultimate demonstration of being a disciple. Earlier, we touched on the story of Ignatius of Antioch who asserts that "only the martyr is a true disciple."[1] This commitment of the early Christians included the price of obeying Jesus to the death. But several developments would change what it cost to be a Christian, the result would not bode well for the practice of real discipleship.

The Price of a Less Costly Christianity: Shallow Congregations

Dietrich Bonhoeffer, arguably the preeminent Twentieth Century thinker on this subject, points to the "secularization" of the church as the beginning of the problem.[2] To consider the validity of this hypothesis we consider the Edicts of Toleration (311) and Milan (313) and the eventual development of Christianity as an official religion by mid-4th century. Accordingly, this 'secularization' would have opened the doors of regular Christian gatherings, which may well have been previously kept quiet due to persecution. This new openness and freedom led to the reconstruction of church buildings after many were destroyed in the persecutions. Today, we commonly refer to a building as a church, rather than the congregation that meets inside. This has created a culture in which we think of 'going to church' rather than the reality that we *are* the church. A side effect of this thinking is that making disciples has often become secondary to the construction and maintenance of the right structure and the form for the weekly meeting. Gatherings of disciples moved from homes into church buildings that grew larger and larger.

A further change in the once illegal, then tolerated, and ultimately official church is that gatherings may have been attended by many who previously would not have been seen at such meetings. This is because of the associated risk during times of persecution, *if* they had even known about them. With new openness and freedom, interested persons might have attended church for business, social or even political motivations. As Constantine became directly involved in Christianity in the mid fourth century, the attraction would have only increased. In response, some left

---

[1] K. H. Rengstorf, "*mathānō.*" in *Theological Dictionary of the New Testament*, ed. Gerhard Kittel and Gerhard Friedrich, trans., abr. ed., ed., Geoffrey W. Bromiley (Grand Rapids: Eerdmans Publishing, 1985), 562.

[2] Dietrich Bonhoeffer, *The Cost of Discipleship* (New York: Simon and Schuster, 1959), Kindle ed., 46. This classic on discipleship is highly influential in the approach of this chapter and will be referred to frequently.

these churches to seek God in isolation. Oxford historian Benedicta Ward, herself a member of an Anglican Community, describes this changing situation. She states that the changes served as "...a further impetus..."[3] for disciples to move to the desert. Ward clarifies that this exodus responds to the situation that emerged as the church was legitimized under Constantine. Once considered rebels and atheists by the empire, these Christians had found a new respectability in the Roman world.[4] Ward asserts that those who fled the world to seek God in the desert were resisting what was becoming, what many call, a cultural Christianity. Bonhoeffer referred to this as a secularized church and this change in status meant that there was a lower cost to adherents. No longer was it dangerous, indeed in some cases, it was now fashionable to be a Christian. This is the beginning of Bonhoeffer's indictment that is so widely known as a church weakened by "cheap grace."[5] A grace that is gained at a small price to the recipient. This low price means that many people have become, cultural Christians.

Today, this idea of the 'Cultural Christian' is well described by Ed Stetzer, a leading thinker on Christianity in America today, Stetzer holds the Billy Graham Chair of Church, Mission, and Evangelism at Wheaton College and serves as executive director of the Billy Graham Center for Evangelism. He explains that "Cultural Christians"[6] are comprised of church goers that consider themselves Christians because of their culture, believing "themselves to be Christians simply because their culture tells them they are."[7] Astonishingly, Stetzer asserts this group represents twenty-five percent of America. The second category, another twenty-five percent of America are what he calls "Congregational Christians."[8] These are people who have a connection to a congregation, through upbringing, marriage and so forth. They attend services but lack real commitment. The final group are

---

[3] Benedicta Ward, *The Desert Fathers: Sayings of the Early Christian Monks* (London, England: Penguin Books Ltd., 2003) Kindle ed., location 149.

[4] Ward, *The Desert Fathers*, location 149.

[5] Cf. Bonhoeffer, *The Cost of Discipleship*, 46.

[6] Ed Stetzer, "The State of the American Church: When Numbers Point to a New Reality," in Evangelical Missions Quarterly, July 2016, https://emqonline.com/node/3520 (accessed 7-11-16).

[7] Stetzer, "The State of the American Church," July 2016.

[8] Stetzer, "The State of the American Church," July 2016.

"Convictional Christians"[9] They live as their faith dictates and are growing in it.[10] They have experienced change.

Bonhoeffer, Ward and Stetzer demonstrate that the situation in twenty-first century West and fourth century Rome have significant similarities. This secularization is not just a phenomenon of the mid-fourth century, it can be observed throughout the history of Christianity. While not in the scope of this project, it would be easy to see the decline of Western culture as related to a low-cost Christianity where freedom is expected and anyone of any commitment level may be considered part of a local church. The result is a weak Church in the West today where the fear of not getting tax breaks from the government is counted as persecution. This secularization was the result of what we will refer to as a church establishment.[11] An establishment that, once legitimacy had been gained in the eyes of the government, would expand. This expansion would be both in numbers of churches and in hierarchy[12] to administrate the growth.[13]

The Changing Meaning of 'Christian'

It may be argued that Bonhoeffer's secularization, illustrated by what we have called established churches, created a climate where the very understanding of what it meant to be a Christian began to change. This is, perhaps, what C. S. Lewis has in mind when he argues that the name 'Christian' has lost its meaning. He points out that the word had come to

---

[9] Stetzer, "The State of the American Church," July 2016.

[10] Stetzer, "The State of the American Church," July 2016.

[11] In the context of this work, the word 'establishment' in referring to churches is more helpful than, say, 'mainline' churches. This is because the problem we are describing is more about the lack of discipleship among the people than the various theological or sociological positions of denominations.

[12] Roger Olson, *The Story of Christian Theology* (Downers Grove, IL: InterVarsity Press, 1999), 124-125. Olson asserts that this development of the hierarchy of the church in the third century was in part a response to persecution. He gives three reasons: a) the need to establish authority after the death of the apostles; b) the need for leadership in the face of persecution; c) the need to deal with theological error.

[13] Olson, *The Story of Christian Theology*, 126. He notes: "Bishop Cornelius of Rome, self-proclaimed pope of the middle of the third century, had 155 clergy of various ranks working under him in Rome."

mean a kind and thoughtful person rather than one who has forsaken all for Jesus.[14] We have asserted that many are counted as Christians for *cultural reasons* since it is part of their upbringing and the expectations of their local culture. These 'cultural Christians' may even recite the creeds and say the prayers in church. As one pastor laments, there is a danger that they are merely 'checking a box' on their weekly inventory which includes practicing Christianity on Sunday morning.[15] They may believe, but demonstrate little conscious dependence on God in everyday life. There is little evidence of obedience to the commands of Jesus let alone any real suffering for His name. Sadly, when one studies the Church worldwide today one easily sees that this is a widespread problem.

Writing about the current state of the global church, missiologist Philip Jenkins analyzes this problem. He asserts that cultural Christians make it difficult to assess the accuracy of reported numbers of members within denominations or movements. This results from the dichotomy between "joining a church" and actual "conversion."[16] To count the people responding to an evangelism event is one thing, to find those who had actually received God's justification is another thing all together. Jenkins was writing about the Southern World of South America and Africa but, as already noted, this assessment is especially true of the West. Indeed, this has become a 'norm' in Western cultures. Why? Perhaps because in so many places, it is no longer dangerous to be a Christian. This freedom and acceptance is in opposition to the counter-cultural mandate that exists in the

---

[14] C. S. Lewis, *Mere Christianity*, (New York: Macmillan, 1952; repr, New York, HarperCollins, 2009) Kindle. The Preface to *Mere Christianity* provides an insightful discussion about the changing meaning of the word 'Christian' and the meaning of words in general. Unless we all know what the other means by the words we use, we are not communicating. We are not to reach too far here, Lewis does not argue explicitly for the kind of distinction between disciple and convert that are found on the pages of this project, yet the very content of that modern classic is filled with essential teachings on being a disciple.

[15] William Copeland, a Virginia pastor and educator has frequently taught his congregation that Christians should not "show up" to "check off a box" on Sunday thus making Sunday church attendance one compartment in an overly busy life that may ignore faithful living the rest of the week.

[16] Philip Jenkins, *The Next Christendom: The Coming of Global Christianity* (New York, Oxford University Press, 2011), Kindle ed., location 1169.

Bible. When churches are so free in a culture, they can, because they are so safe and comfortable, begin to focus on their buildings, comfort, audio-visual presentations and musical styles. The next step is to lessen the time given to the preaching of the Scripture to give more time for singing, which has become synonymous with 'worship.' These aspects of their weekly services have become a part of their identity; a kind of performance philosophy has set in. Committed disciples will be more interested in human needs for Christ than how well the weekly service production goes. But when the focus of the church is on the growing attendance at the weekly service rather than 'disciple making', these issues dominate. A means has become dangerously close to becoming the end. Indeed, why would the New Testament warn us about all the suffering that the church would endure if it would become such a culturally legitimized, established, 'normal' institution? How can the church speak into, and often against, the culture when it has become such a part of the culture? It can't. Its influence is muted when it begins to become a thermometer rather than a thermostat. A thermometer simply shows the temperature, a thermostat initiates actions that change the temperature. In this situation, local churches risk reflecting the culture rather than being a prophetic voice calling for biblical living. Thus, Bonhoeffer's hypothesis is in line with what Ward stated earlier about the Desert Fathers as discipleship moved to the relative obscurity of the monastery.

Seeking God Outside Cultural Christianity

Monasteries, continuing with Bonhoeffer's hypothesis, became the primary places of discipleship. He notes that Church leadership viewed the monastic movement to demonstrate the existence of discipleship in an increasingly secularized church.[17] In the desert, there was a real emphasis on seeking God and the development of life together. Indeed, one may see that the life of discipleship might flourish in such an atmosphere.[18] Communities

---

[17] Bonhoeffer, *The Cost of Discipleship*, 46.

[18] The monastic movement (including perhaps the Desert Fathers), however, has its questioners. In his helpful and important work, *The Divine Embrace*, Robert Webber questions monasticism on the basis that it is too Platonic (cf. 46ff). While Webber's perspective is shared by many in evangelicalism, we find that though his book is helpful, he goes too far in his assessment. He is arguing for what he thinks of as a renewed biblical spirituality. His work is valuable and deserves the attention of anyone

of disciples were eventually established where they could live apart from the world in a life of obedience, serving, and, in many places, copying Scripture. In such a context, one can see real potential for disciple making. Indeed, one of the great finds of the 18th century was in the Holy Monastery of Saint Catherine in Sinai, where the oldest existing complete New Testament, Codex Sinaiticus was located. It was the monastic scribal practices that preserved the text of Scriptures like this. Bibles that would be lost for centuries and then discovered during an awakening of biblical scholarship. These ancient manuscripts emerged, in part, from archeological expeditions, a process that began in the 18th century and continues to the present day. Bonhoeffer's assertion is insightful with the realization that if one wished to be a true disciple, the monastery was a place to go.

Yet, the move to the monastery was not without its challenges. It potentially created a new roadblock to 'disciple making.' If discipleship, as we infer from Bonhoeffer, lives solely or primarily in the monastery, and the world was outside, how could disciples effect the world? British apologist and philosopher, Os Guinness called this separation between the church and the world a distortion between vocation and calling.[19] One may understand this distortion when comparing that, over time, the place of the clergy in culture becomes higher than the place of the laity. The clergy have a higher and more noble calling, while the laity, no matter their own real piety, are of a lower position. Catholic theologian Keith Egan describes a narrowing of discipleship. "Eventually in the tradition, a popular notion of discipleship restricted this model for Christian life to religious and clergy."[20] Baptist historian Roger Olson agrees and points out that the role of the laity diminished during these years, this growing reliance on clergy exacerbated the decline of disciple making among the people in the gathering of local congregations. Olson notes that the more the church established the importance of the clergy, "the role of the laity tended to diminish. At the beginning of the third century lay Christians... ...often performed baptisms and led in worship, including the Lord's Supper. ... All that changed with the

---

interested in spiritual development in the practice of discipleship. Robert Webber, *The Divine Embrace* (Grand Rapids, MI: Baker Books, 2006).

[19] Os Guinness, *The Call: Finding and Fulfilling the Central Purpose of Your Life* (Nashville, TN: Thomas Nelson, Inc., 2003), Kindle ed., 48.

[20] Keith Egan, "Discipleship" in *HarperCollins Encyclopedia of Catholicism*, 1995 ed.

clericalization process."[21] Historian W. H. C. Frend explains the transition.

> The liturgy was becoming more formal and the penitential system more exact. The administration of both had become a clerical preserve. At the beginning of the [third] century the laity in the church at Carthage might still expect to take an individual part in the service, to 'prophecy,' or sing something of one's own composition. The laity could also baptize, and this seems to have been the tradition in Rome also. By mid-century this had changed. Cyprian never speaks of baptism by laity in his many references to the subject. The celebration of the mysteries was the prerogative of priests alone.[22]

As the professionals increased their own influence and control, the laity had less and less involvement. Thus, we think again of Bonhoeffer and his hypothesis that disciple making only occurred in the monastery. The possibility decreased that those outside church and cloister would be exposed to a committed life of following and obeying Jesus. Yet, it is important to affirm that the monasteries did maintain the light of disciple making for many centuries. Evidence of this may be found in the writing of the Desert Fathers. We turn to these writings to help us understand disciple making. As Paul urges. "keep your eyes on those who walk according to the example you have in us."[23] We may look to and learn from these who have gone before us.

Applicative Questions

What lessons about cultural Christianity in your context have you struggled with?

What are ways in which your own ministry is susceptible to secularization? How could meeting on a regular basis with a person who is a cultural Christian help them move toward becoming a disciple?

---

[21] Olson, *The Story of Christian Theology*, 126-7.
[22] W. H. C. Frend, *The Rise of Christianity* (Philadelphia: Fortress, 1984), 407.
[23] Philippians 3:17.

CHAPTER EIGHT

DESERT FATHERS, AUGUSTINE AND AQUINAS

The Desert Fathers Reject Secularization

The Desert Fathers were a movement that began early (circa. 2nd Century) in the history of Christianity. Individuals went into the deserts of Palestine, Egypt and elsewhere seeking God at a deeper level. As time passed, individuals began to help one another, this gathering was the beginning of the monastic movement. Well known leaders like Antony (251-356) and lesser known ones like Arsenius (350-445) became advisors to other monks.[1] Their ministry also extended to those who came from population centers to visit and receive counsel, then, in person, as now, through writings. Their teachings were sought out for spiritual development. This was and remains helpful in disciple making. As these people sought the freedom to wait for God in solitude. They hoped to enter in the fullness of life in the Father, Son and Holy Spirit.[2]

The collected sayings of these leaders who sought God in the desert are the evidence of their disciple making. They gave counsel to those who sought them out to learn how to know God more deeply. This occurred when younger monks sought out the wisdom of those who were older. As others came to live nearby, groups would combine efforts for counsel, shared meals and provisions. They began helping one another to follow Christ as His students.[3] Disciple making was occurring among hermits and within these

---

[1] Peter Gorg, *The Desert Fathers: Anthony and the Beginnings of Monasticism*, trans. Michael J. Miller (San Francisco: Ignatius Press, 2011), ix. Peter Gorg describes the early Christian monk in *The Desert Fathers* as one who "…knows only one goal: the absolute submission of his whole being to God by imitating Christ."

[2] Benedicta Ward, *The Desert Fathers: Sayings of the Early Christian Monks* (London, England: Penguin Books Ltd., 2003) Kindle ed., viii-ix.

[3] For a greater understanding of the development of early monasticism, both spiritually and practically, see Ward's excellent Introduction in *The Desert Fathers*, cf. fn. 60.

developing monasteries. The collected writings and sayings of the Desert Fathers would remain influential in the monastery and would have influence in the more established church as well.

The Influence of The Desert Fathers

Over time the counsel of the elders, among them the sayings of Antony, were published broadly to help many on their path to God. These devotional writings may be more like the genre of Proverbs than of the Psalms or Epistles. The thinking and traditions of these Desert Fathers continued most clearly in what became Eastern Christianity, which is, perhaps, more widely known as Orthodox Christianity, and less well known as Byzantine Christianity. The history, theology and practice of Eastern Christianity take a somewhat different path than Western Christianity and deserve consideration as there are principles herein that show discipleship at work. The study of their theology, practice and politics (the later resulting in national and ethnic churches), while fascinating, would not lend to our study. However, for those of us who interact in cultures affected by Eastern practices, to gain some understanding of them will be profitable.

The thinking and practices of Eastern Christian discipleship may be observed in the work of Irenaeus (130-202), Origen (185-254)[4] and, especially Athanasius (296-373). It would be particularly helpful for the disciple to consider Athanasius' work, *On the Incarnation*. There are few better examples of early spiritual development writing. Orthodox theologian Bradley Nassif explains the importance of the Eastern doctrine of the incarnation: "It would not be an overstatement to assert that the entire history of Byzantine theology from the fourth to the fourteenth centuries constitutes an extended exegesis of the soteriological meaning of the incarnation...."[5] This is of particular interest as one seeks to understand the ongoing process of becoming like Christ, or, as referred to in Eastern Orthodox practice, 'theosis' (deification or divinization). This doctrine is at the heart of Orthodox spiritual development.

---

[4] Roger Olson, *The Story of Christian Theology* (Downers Grove, IL: InterVarsity Press, 1999), 112, cf. 186ff.

[5] Bradley Nassif, "Are Eastern Orthodoxy and Evangelicalism Compatible? Yes" in *Three Views on Eastern Orthodoxy and Evangelicalism*, ed. James Stamoolis, Counterpoints: Exploring Theology (Grand Rapids: Zondervan, 2004), p.45.

One can see the widespread application to discipleship.

Chorbishop Seely Beggiani describes theosis, referring to fourth century father, St. Ephrem the Syrian (306-373), whose teaching on the matter are twofold. He states that God is "mystery and the call to become like God."[6] Beggiani clarifies that "at no time in our religious experience do we possess God; it is he that possesses us."[7] This articulates that it is a work of God in us more than anything we may do. One may see Paul's doctrine of sanctification in Romans 6-8 in this teaching. Dumitru Staniloae states that divination is a lifelong process beginning "at Baptism, and stretches out all along the whole of man's spiritual ascent."[8] The process is the work of God, the Holy Spirit.[9] Two other crucial aspects of Eastern spiritual practices of spiritual development, are the Jesus Prayer and the use of icons.

The use of the Jesus Prayer (Lord Jesus Christ, Son of God, Savior, have mercy on me, a sinner.) is viewed as a helpful way to practice Paul's admonition to "pray without ceasing."[10] St. Theophan the Recluse notes that the "most experienced men of spiritual life who were enlightened by God found this to be the one simple and all-effective means for confirming the spirit in all spiritual activities.[11] In the Russian Orthodox story "The Way of a Pilgrim"[12] one may see how the Jesus Prayer is a key discipline. In it, a pilgrim seeks and finds instruction on the spiritual life. He then embarks on a pilgrimage of seeking God with the primary tool being the Jesus Prayer.

The second discipline is, what is perhaps the most well-known

---

[6] Seely Beggiani, *Introduction to Eastern Christian Spirituality: The Syriac Tradition* (London: University of Scranton Press, 1991), 13.

[7] Beggiani, *Introduction to Eastern Christian Spirituality*, 13. It is at this juncture that Webber's assessment provides important questions regarding the value of these teachings, cf. fn. 73 above. He provides a helpful discussion of theosis in *Divine Embrace, 41ff.*

[8] Dumitru Staniloae, *Orthodox Spirituality*, trans. Archimandrite Jerome and Otilia Kloos (South Canaan, PA: St. Tikhon's Orthodox Theological Seminary Press, 2002), 363.

[9] Dumitru Staniloae, *Orthodox Spirituality*, 363.

[10] 1 Thessalonians 5:17.

[11] St. Theophan the Recluse, *The Path to Salvation* (Safford, AZ: St. Paisius Monastery, 2006), 257-258.

[12] "The Way of a Pilgrim," trans. Nina A Toumanova, in G. P. Fedotov, ed., *A Treasury of Russian Spiritually* (New York: Harper Torchbooks, 1965; repr., The Way of A Pilgrim, Mineola, NY: Dover Publications, 2003), Kindle ed., 281ff.

Orthodox practice, the use of icons. Nassif describes the basis for their use.

> Building on Scripture and the conclusions reached by the Council of
> Chalcedon nearly three hundred years earlier, the Orthodox drew out
> the implications of the incarnation for Christian art, arguing that
> icons function as educational tools, models of saints' lives, witnesses
> to the ultimate transfiguration of the cosmos, and, above all,
> dogmatic confessions in lines and colors that 'the Word became flesh
> and made his dwelling among us' (John 1:14).[13]

Scholar Constantine Cavarnos lists several uses for icons. He notes that they beautify the building, provide teaching about the Christian life, remind the people of faith, offer a focus to holy living like unto those represented, help to transform and provide a method of "worship and veneration."[14] A helpful resource in the understanding of and use of icons from a more Western perspective may be found in Henri J. M. Nouwen's *Behold the Beauty of the Lord*.[15] These three elements are at the heart of Orthodox spiritual development. Their key aim being the journey of living for God. For our purposes, we will return to further consideration of Christian disciplines in Chapter Seven.

These writings provide us with several lessons. First, we should seek those more experienced than ourselves in the way of the Lord. Secondly, we may well serve the Kingdom by recording our spiritual reflections for the benefit of others and finally, that we should be willing to engage with others in fellow disciple making. We never know how our meager efforts might be used by God to draw others unto Himself. Today, many share their insights with others and have a wide following on their websites, blogs, Twitter and Facebook.

The stories of the Desert Fathers had a powerful effect on their readers, many of whom would emerge as useful instruments of God. Ward

---

[13] Nassif, "Are Eastern Orthodoxy and Evangelicalism Compatible? Yes," 55.

[14] Constantine Cavarnos, "The Functions of Icons," *Orthodox Christian Information Center*,
http://orthodoxinfo.com/general/icon_function.aspx (accessed 10-23-16).

[15] Henri J. M. Nouwen, *Behold the Beauty of the Lord* (Notre Dame, IN: Ave Maria Press, 1987).

recounts a conversation between young friends in Milan in 386 who were discussing the news that two friends had been inspired by the life of Antony to leave civil service to become monks. One participant in this conversation excused himself to be alone and consider what he had heard. What he then heard is now famous. 'Take up and read, take up and read.'[16] This, of course, is the conversion of Augustine (354-430). One may even assert that after the Apostles and the Bible, no one is more influential than Augustine. Because of his theological significance, he is lauded by Reformers and Roman Catholics alike. Historian Justo Gonzalez describes the influence of the Bishop of Hippo.

> Augustine is the end of one era as well as the beginning of another. He is the last of the ancient Christian fathers, and the forerunner of medieval theology. The main currents of ancient theology converged in him, and from him flow the rivers, not only of medieval scholasticism, but also of sixteenth-century Protestant Theology.[17]

But how does Augustine enhance discussion about disciple making?

In his 60s, during the time he was writing *The City of God*, Augustine received a letter from a younger man by the name of Laurence. The reply of the bishop describes Laurence's request. "It is your desire, as you wrote, to have from me a book, a sort of enchiridion, as it might be called--something to have 'at hand'--that deals with your questions."[18] Realizing the importance of answers to probing questions, Augustine writes thirty-three chapters of wisdom to Laurence. The text reads at once like a combination of proverbs, theological letters and philosophical musings. It is as though we might be listening in on a conversation about how to follow God. Contemporary to the great thinker was Jerome (347-420), an important scholar who led the effort to translate the Vulgate.

In a correspondence between Jerome and Augustine we find conflict and resolution. Theologian Gerard Jacobitz juxtaposes the men: "There could be no greater contrast in personalities than between Jerome and Augustine of

---

[16] Ward, *The Desert Fathers*, location 329.

[17] Justo Gonzalez, *A History of Christian Thought*, vol. 2 (Nashville, TN: Abingdon, 1971), 15.

[18] Augustine, *Enchiridion On Faith, Hope, and Love*, ed. and trans. Albert Outler (Dallas TX: Southern Methodist University, 1955), Kindle ed., location 55.

Hippo. Great as he was a theologian, Augustine was perhaps an even greater pastor, blessed with that most important asset of any effective minister, a broken ego."[19] As the events unfold, Augustine wrote to protest a change in the translator's process. Previously, Jerome had been translating the Old Testament into Latin using the Greek Septuagint. Seeking to work from the original language, Jerome had changed to the Hebrew Scriptures. Augustine considered this ill advised. He argued that the research behind the Septuagint, the Second Century BC Greek translation of the Old Testament, was better than Jerome or his assistants could surpass. Augustine also disagreed with an interpretation from 2 Peter and challenged Jerome on this point. This first letter was lost, but the second letter did arrive in the hands, not of Jerome, but in those of some in Rome who published the document. In this indirect and public manner, Jerome received the complaints of Augustine. Jerome responded directly with serious protest of his own. In his reply, we see that Augustine understood the importance of relationship with the elder scholar. He writes, this time not as a protesting theologian, but as a pastor seeking reconciliation. In this, we see the importance of friendship to Augustine who writes eloquently on the importance of friends:

> I admit that I can easily rest myself to their love, especially when I am worn out by the scandals of this world and I can rest in their love, free from cares and convinced that God is there; I can safely cast myself on him and rest safely in him. In my freedom from anxiety I have absolutely no fear of that uncertainty of the future, inherent in man's weakness, which I was lamenting earlier in the letter. When I feel that a man is burning with Christian love which has made him a loyal friend, whatever plans or thoughts of mine which I entrust to him, I know that I am entrusting them not to a mere man but to God, in whom my friend remains so as to be what he is; for God is love and anyone who remains in love remains in God and God in him.[20]

From this attitude, stating the importance of friendship, we may learn much

---

[19] Gerard Jacobitz, "The Epistolary Correspondence of Saints Jerome and Augustine and the Expansion of the Rule of Saint Benedict from 66 to 73 Chapters" in *American Benedictine Review*, Vol. 63, Issue 4 (Dec 2012), 384-417.
[20] Jacobitz, "The Epistolary Correspondence," 392.

from Augustine. We learn that friendship may not be just a fruit of disciple making but a key component of the process as will become apparent in Chapter Eight. Jacobitz elaborates: "For Augustine, friends are companions who, insofar as they rest in God, speak the truth with authority. A friend might even be the better judge of one's own character than one's self."[21] This is an apt description of the fruit of a disciple making conversation. Helping one another see the flaws inherent in one's own fallen nature and pointing one another to the God who redeems that nature. From Augustine, we see the importance of cultivating friendships that God uses to bring us closer to Him. From this example of friendship as read in the record of Augustine, we turn to the work of his correspondent, who is, perhaps, best known for his work, the Vulgate.

Jerome and The Vulgate

Jerome, while serving as a papal Secretary, began a groundbreaking project of translating the Bible into Latin, the official language of the day. His important work would last for 23 years beginning in 382 and continuing until 405. This was not the first translation into Latin. Jacobitz asserts that there were plenty of translations, but none of them were well done.[22] Upon completion, the Latin Bible (Vulgate) would make Scripture more accessible because it was in a common language. There would be greater availability of Scripture and eventually, as the rites were made uniform, one could travel anywhere that the established church reigned, and be familiar with the service of worship. That traveler could hear the same Bible read and the same liturgy sung in any church. Theoretically, this should facilitate the spreading of the gospel and it is noted that the reach of the Church continued to advance geographically. In Jerome's work, however, we discover a challenge: a de-emphasizing of 'disciple making' and the elevation of 'teaching' in our key text, Matthew 28:19.[23]

Swiss theologian Ulrich Luz, like France in his commentaries on

---

[21] Jacobitz, "The Epistolary Correspondence," 403. Jacobitz notes that "This was Augustine's point in Ep. 73" referring to the long quote on page 76.

[22] Jacobitz, "The Epistolary Correspondence," 393.

[23] Cf. Christopher de Hamel, *The Book. A History of the Bible* (London: Phaidon Press, 2001), 12ff.

Matthew, places significant emphasis on 'disciple making' in his understanding of Matthew's complete message. In the Vulgate, μαθητεύσατε (*mathēteusate)*, was not translated 'make disciples;' Jerome chose the word *docete* (teach). This translation is not wrong as much as it is an incomplete concept. Luz asserts the significance therein was that this "obliterated both the uniqueness of the Matthean ecclesiology of discipleship as well as the dominance of it in praxis (v. 20a)"[24] This is significant because it places the emphasis on teaching, rather than disciple making. Clearly, teaching is key to disciple making but as will be argued later, is only one aspect of the process. As we seek to establish, disciple making moves knowledge from the head to the heart and from knowing to understanding.

To understand why this is considered problematic, we consider the organized instruction for new believers, the catechism. This instruction was provided so that they may be brought into the church through baptism or confirmation. The problem develops as one must pass a test administered by the church to confirm faith while never actually living in obedience to the teachings of Jesus. If all one must do is memorize knowledge to pass a verbal test, then the true life of following Jesus is lost. For more than a millennium, per our hypothesis, the die was cast. Superficiality would flourish.

Papacy, Clergy and the Kingdoms of Men

In the centuries that followed, the story of the church was marred by intrigue, politics, land grabs, and the Crusades. The Papacy rose in influence and power. Corruptions and conflicts occurred through the years, all of which are outside the scope of this inquiry. But the mention of such events provides some understanding why individual disciple making largely fell by the wayside except, as Bonhoeffer stated and as we have illustrated, in the desert and monastery. These centuries of power and politics proved problematic to the condition of the clergy and therefore the individual parishes. But scholarship continued and Scholasticism emerged.[25] Related to this movement, the

---

[24] Ulrich Luz, *Matthew 21-28: A Commentary* (Minneapolis, Minn.: Augsburg Fortress, 2005), 625.

[25] Scholasticism was a movement that began circa. 1100 in which universities emphasized Aristotelian logic and traditional doctrine. Thomas Aquinas is perhaps the most well-known of the school men, as they were also

university emerged. It might be reasonable to assume a lack of emphasis on discipleship but that would be oversimplifying the issue. Indeed, the most prominent figure of Scholasticism, Thomas Aquinas (1225-1274), displayed a deep desire to know and rely on God and to help others do the same.

Aquinas as Disciple-Maker

A helpful description of the life and work of Aquinas is found in the 1959 work *The Life of Saint Thomas Aquinas* by Dominican Kenelm Foster.[26] In this volume, is a translation of *"Life of St. Thomas Aquinas"* by Bernard Gui. Here, the reader sees the great doctor of the church in his natural habitat, the university and the church. Gui notes that Thomas preached the "word of God with singular grace and power without indulging in far-fetched reasoning"[27] he did so in his mother tongue and moved the congregation to a response. Thomas worked alongside colleagues and students some of whom served as his faithful secretaries. Among those was Reginald. He was a companion and confessor to Thomas from the early 1260s until Aquinas' death in 1274. It was Reginald for whom Aquinas wrote *Compendium Theologiae*,[28] a work written to provide answers to theological questions. Upon reading the collection, we may easily see these responses as a form of disciple making. There is no doubt that Thomas left an indelible mark on the church, and on the disciples with whom he collaborated. Part of that mark was a brand of what we would call mysticism. Historian Jean-Pierre Torrell

---

known. Whether fair or not, scholastics are generally known for arguing over how many angels could dance on the head of a pin.

[26] Kenelm Foster, O.P., trans. and ed. *The Life of Saint Thomas Aquinas: Biographical Documents* (London: Longmans, Green and Co. 1959).

[27] Bernard Gui, "Life of St. Thomas Aquinas" in Kenelm Foster, O.P., trans. and ed. *The Life of Saint Thomas Aquinas: Biographical Documents* (London: Longmans, Green and Co. 1959), 47.

[28] Jean-Pierre Torrell, O.P., *Saint Thomas Aquinas Vol. 1, The Person and His Work,* trans. Robert Royal (Washington D.C.: The Catholic University of America Press 1996), 49. This two-volume work when paired with Foster provides insight into the spiritual heart behind the immense theological writing. Of further help into this aspect of our inquiry is "St. Thomas Aquinas: Theologian and Mystic" in Jean-Pierre Torrell, O.P., *Christ and Spirituality in St. Thomas Aquinas,* trans. Bernhard Blankenhorn, O.P., (Washington D.C.: The Catholic University of America Press, 2011), 1-20.

describes his mysticism as an interaction with God. According to Torrell, Aquinas' theology is not centered in speculation about God but rooted in God, his mercy and his love. Theologians must return to God as source of love and theology.[29] It is apparent that Aquinas depended on his deep relationship with God for his theology.

Thus, theological understanding is both contemplative and God centered. Fellow disciples should be urging one another on to deeper biblical understanding of God through Bible reading, prayer and study. We may see this illustrated by an occasion when Aquinas was struggling with a text from Isaiah. For some days and then after prayer and fasting, the understanding of the text came and Aquinas understood. Gui completes the narrative as Thomas calls for his secretary to arise, bring a lamp and join him for dictation. Reginald reported that Thomas' dictation was as though he read form a commentary.[30] Aquinas sought the power of God as a theologian while making disciples through his writing and the tutelage of his students and colleagues. We may take from Aquinas the reminder that endeavoring to do theology is critical, but that the theology must be centered on God through the Bible, and that God may meet us and enlighten us through relationship. Aquinas the great theologian was also Aquinas the great seeker to know God. One may think here of J. I. Packer who deftly distinguishes between knowing about God and knowing God.[31]

Some 250 years later another cleric and teacher emerged, one who would wrestle with mysticism but reject it. This thinker, 500 years ago, was the match that lit the Reformation torch, Martin Luther.

---

[29] Jean-Pierre Torrell, *Saint Thomas Aquinas Vol. 2, Spiritual Master*, trans. Robert Royal (Washington D.C.: The Catholic University of America Press, 2003), 11-12.

[30] Gui, "Life of St. Thomas Aquinas," 38.

[31] Cf. J. I. Packer, *Knowing God* (Downers Grove, IL: InterVarsity Press, 1973).

Applicative Questions

Like the sayings of the Desert Fathers to Augustine, every era has had its 'devotional writers.' What is the danger of reliance on these helpful books? Do you find yourself drawn more readily to these human texts rather than to Scripture?

In recent decades, many Evangelicals have discovered the value of collections of prayers to help them develop their own prayers. Prayer books were widely used by those who could afford them in centuries past. How could reading the prayers of others help you? Conversely, how could they deter your growth in prayer?

As you consider your friends, what are the commonalities that have drawn you together? If you are in full time ministry, do you have friends? Augustine and Jerome had their vocation in common. In his letter to Jerome we see Augustine's heart for friendship. In his *Enchiridion,* we may also see his desire to nurture discipleship among his friends. Consider your own friends, what are ways that you help can nurture their personal discipleship and they yours?

CHAPTER NINE

SEARCHING FOR DISCIPLE MAKING IN THE REFORMATION

In what follows, we examine lives of several figures, two from the Reformation and one Pietist. From there we will move rapidly to the twentieth century and to, perhaps, the most influential Christian of that century. In our ongoing quest to deepen our understanding of Jesus' use of *mathēteusate*, we begin the chapter with further historical information about its translation.

Getting Back to the Original

Because of his work on Scripture, it is important to mention the groundbreaking work of Desiderius Erasmus of Rotterdam (1466-1536) who restored the Greek New Testament as well as made many needed changes to the Vulgate.[1] In this pivotal act of reconstruction, the result of his work was *Novum Instrumentum*. In this document, Erasmus used the Greek word μαθητεύσατε in Matthew 28:19. It is intriguing that, in his corrected version of the Latin, he maintained the translation to *docete*. Agreeing with the translation from a millennium earlier, per our hypothesis, would impact Bible translations until the late 19th century.

As various reformers translated the Bible into their vernaculars, it is apparent that most followed not just Erasmus' Greek New Testament, but his

---

[1] More than a century earlier John Wycliffe, the 14th century English reformer, influenced Czech Jan Hus and thus the Moravians. Wycliffe was important in the history translation of the Bible into English, and into vernaculars in general, but he does not enter this specific discussion because he relied largely, if not completely on the Vulgate. Thus, without the Greek text, he would not have known about the unfortunate variation produced by Jerome 1000 years earlier. Nonetheless, his impact on Pietism and thus discipleship is significant. His protests caused his suppression and eventual death by the church.

commentary on the Greek text and corrections to the Vulgate.[2] William Tyndale (1494-1536) followed Erasmus and used 'teach' in his 1526 English New Testament. Tyndale's work was, of course, that upon which the *King James Version* was largely based. In the English-speaking world, this translation would serve to unify the English language itself. This translation would remain in place until modern translation work began in the late 19th and early 20th centuries. We argue that this translation is highly influential in emphasizing 'proclamation' which would be a key to the great 'reach the world in our lifetime' movements that began in the early 20th century and continued until today.[3] We will return to this discussion later.

Meanwhile Martin Luther (1483-1546) was wrestling not just with God but with the practices of the church. Many of his questions resulted, at least in part, from a reaction to Mysticism. Luther developed both theologically and spiritually under the mentoring of Johann von Staupitz. He assigned the sermons of Johann Tauler and the *Theologia Germanica* (then considered the work of Tauler).[4] It was not just the reading of and accepting of Tauler's brand of mysticism, it was Luther's questioning. Indeed, the influence of the mystic's work on Luther, argues Steven Ozment, was formative in a "hermeneutical breakthrough" as Luther rejected Tauler's essential presuppositions on humanity and the notion of being.[5] It was Luther's critical analysis of his reading that formed him. In this way Staupitz used Scripture and human authors to help move Luther from his theological

---

[2] Cf. Christopher de Hamel, *The Book. A History of the Bible* (London: Phaidon Press, 2001), 12ff, 216ff.

[3] These movements came in tandem with the great missionary conferences of the twentieth century that began in Edinburgh, Scotland in 1910 and continue today, the latest being Cape Town, 2010. These conferences and the goals set therein essentially share a common goal: to proclaim the gospel and convert the nations. This was a great endeavor. Yet, we ask here, is it a truncated view of the Great Commission?

[4] David Bagchi, "Martin Luther: 'Confessional' Theologian" in *The Expository Times*, Vol. 126(2), 55-57.

[5] Steven E. Ozment "An Aid to Luther's Marginal Comments on Johannes Tauler's Sermons," in *The Harvard Theological Review*, Vol. 63, No. 2 (April., 1970), http://www.jstor.org/stable/ 1509029 (accessed 12 June 2016).

darkness. Once his enlightenment arrived, Luther followed Jesus absolutely without concern for cost.[6]

Luther had seen through an ecclesiastical fog that had developed and the resulting works righteousness theologies[7] that rampaged through Europe. This resulted in the convergence in the collecting of money for indulgences. His theological challenge to these myriad corruptions were the 95 theses. Which are, as Reformation scholar David Bagchi clarifies, "an invitation to an academic debate, not a manifesto for revolution."[8] This list of grievances created a storm around the monk. The great turmoil would prove him willing to forsake his life in the cloister and academy to follow Christ into the outside world. As Luther left the priory, would disciple making made its way out as well? Would the laity benefit from this change?

Luther's Letters as Disciple Making

In 1535 Luther's his barber asked for advice on how to pray. He answered with a letter that was later published as *A Simple Way to Pray*.[9] This

---

[6] Cf. Bonhoeffer, *The Cost of Discipleship*, 7.

[7] Some of which remained because of the influence of Pelagius and those who, to one degree or another, incorporated his high view of man which therefore led to a too high view of man's merit. This led to a confusion in the theologies of many as to how man may be reconciled to God. Indeed, Luther's influences included leaders with these views. For a helpful, but very technical, discussion, see Steven E. Ozment "Homo Spiritualis: A Comparative study of the Anthropology of Johannes Tauler, Jean Gerson and Martin Luther (1509-16) in the Context of their Theological Thought" in *Studies in Medieval and Reformation Thought*, vol. 6, ed. Heiko Oberman (Leiden, GY: E. J. Brill, 1969).

[8] David Bagchi, "Martin Luther: 'Confessional' Theologian" in *The Expository Times*, Vol. 126(2), 53-62. Cf. In this thorough but concise essay, Bagchi takes the technical basis laid by Ozment and applies it to what may be understood as a practical theology, or better, a pastoral theology. This pastoral theology helps lay a theological foundation for the disciple making being presented here. This disciple making is indeed a pastoral activity, but not restricted to the professional clergy.

[9] Martin Luther, *A Simple Way to Pray*, Matthew C. Harrison, trans. (St. Louis, MO: Concordia Publishing House, 2012).

little book was an instructive act of 'disciple making' on Luther's part.[10] It remains a helpful resource on developing disciples. In Luther, we see a pastor who was a theologian who asserted that one becomes a theologian through living, "dying and being damned." It is through life and all its struggles that "God's word takes root and grows in you, the devil will harry you, and will make a real doctor of you, and by his assaults will teach you to seek and love God's Word."[11] Bagchi provides a helpful summation of Luther's practical theology. Indeed, he provides us with a helpful description of what fellow disciples should be engaged in: wrestling with God together and helping one another when the devil assails. Luther's letter to his barber was not an isolated incident. Bagchi describes the nearly 3000 extant letters of Luther to a wide variety of correspondents. He states that these letters were about all aspects of regular life, from "a daughter pursuing an unsuitable attachment, a nagging wife, a violent husband, or a poltergeist sharing one's house,[12]" about these and other issues, "one wrote to Dr. Luther for help."[13]

In his writing, Luther's disciple making was broad and personal. He invested in the people to whom he wrote, it was through his life and his prolific output of writing that he influenced people to personal discipleship. This is disciple making. To our textual question, we turn to his sermons and theological writings to ascertain if Dr. Luther will help us in our search for deeper understanding of our word from Matthew's Gospel.

In *Martin Luther's Works*, looking for his thoughts on our key text, we discover that we are surprisingly limited to lectures on the "The Sermon on

---

[10] Aquinas was inspired by the structure of Augustine's *Enchiridion on Faith, Hope and Love* (cf Jean-Pierre Torrell, O.P. *Saint Thomas Aquinas Vol. 2 Spiritual Master*, 323). Luther too followed a similar outline to help his barber and others gain insight into developing more meaningful prayer. Indeed, we may observe that these three great thinkers understood the importance of simplicity. This is an apt lesson for any disciple-maker.

[11] Bagchi, "Martin Luther: 'Confessional' Theologian," 55. Bagchi cites both "*Operationes in Psalmsos* (1519-21), on Ps. 5:11, in WA 5:163.28-29." and "Luther's preface to the 1539 edition of his German writings, WA 50:660.8-10." The first quote also finds use in Philip Jacob Spener, *Pia Desideria*, trans. and ed. Theodore Tappert (Minneapolis, MN: Fortress Press, 1964), Kindle ed. The reader is reminded of a similar heart in Aquinas, cf. Chapter Five.

[12] Bagchi, "Martin Luther: 'Confessional' Theologian," 59.

[13] Bagchi, "Martin Luther: 'Confessional' Theologian," 59.

the Mount" and "The Magnificat." There are neither commentary nor lectures on the gospel of Matthew. We must look elsewhere in his work to glean how he uses the word. Of five references to Matthew 28:19 in the index to *Works*, one citation quotes the English translation "...go and preach the gospel."[14] This quote concerns an unrelated subject. Our inference is that the emphasis was on 'preach' rather than 'make disciples.' The other four occurrences are simply parenthetic prooftexts for other topics with no direct relevance to our subject. This is a small, single piece of evidence. But the fact that the word 'disciple' is absent from the index for the multivolume *Luther's Works* allows one the inference that his focus was on teaching with no explicit reference to the words disciple or disciple making. There is no doubt that Luther's life and ministry facilitated countless disciples, but his writings are of little help in our etymological quest. It is intriguing that he did not teach about discipleship while his example speaks volumes. One may rightly conclude that his life and writing manifested disciple making while he didn't explicitly teach about the word. That said, we turn to the great reformer from France.

Calvin's Institutes as a Resource for Disciple Making

In his commentary on the Synoptics, John Calvin (1509-1564), writing about Matthew 28:19, states that "they are first taught simply to teach."[15] From his comment may presume that Calvin relies on the work of Erasmus for his work on the text. In the writing of these key reformers, the word or even the explicit concept of disciple, disciple making or discipleship are largely absent. Yet, they were disciples making disciples. Calvin provided helpful disciple making counsel in *Institutes of the Christian Religion*.

In the introduction, titled "Subject Matter of the Present Work from the French edition of 1560,"[16] it is clear the *Institutes* are designed to make disciples. The method of work is to pose and answer questions. One may see

---

[14] Martin Luther, "Word and Sacrament," in *Luther's Works*, Vol. 38, trans. and eds., Helmut Lehmann and Martin Lehmann (Saint Louis, MO: Concordia Publishing House,1958), 161.

[15] John Calvin, *Commentary on a Harmony of the Evangelists*. vol. 3, trans. William Pringle (Edinburgh, 1846), 383.

[16] John Calvin, *Institutes of the Christian Religion*, ed. John T. McNeill, trans. Ford Lewis Battles, The Library of Christian Classics, vol. 20, (Philadelphia, PA: The Westminster Press, 1960), 583.

that the entirety of the work is designed for "teaching them to observe all that I have commanded you."[17] Our key text, Matthew 28:19, is used 15 times, yet all are in the context of teaching and baptism. Calvin does not discuss disciple making. Yet, as material for fellow disciples to read and discuss, this work has a wealth of practical theology as well as general theology as the following will demonstrate.

We assert the centrality of reading the Bible in disciple making. On the relation between the Bible and the heart and mind, Calvin asserts that developing both is essential.

> It now remains to pour into the heart itself what the mind has absorbed. For the Word of God is not received by faith if it flits about in the top of the brain, but when it takes root in the depth of the heart that it may be an invincible defense to withstand and drive off the stratagems of temptation.[18]

As such, Calvin teaches us that as fellow disciples read, know and apply Scripture we must move it from the head to the heart and then outward in the way we live. A true theologian like Paul, Calvin understood the importance of the heart.

For fellow disciples, ministering to the heart is crucial. To aid the heart's development we must understand the battle that we are in with sin and the enemy. This battle must not be fought alone. Calvin urges mutual confession in a section refuting the teaching of the 'confessional' of Roman Catholicism.

> "Let us take the apostles view, which is simple and open: namely, that we should lay our infirmities on one another's breasts, to receive among ourselves mutual counsel, mutual compassion, and mutual consolation. Then, as we are aware of our brothers' infirmities, let us pray to God for these."[19]

---

[17] Matthew 28:20.

[18] Calvin, *Institutes of the Christian Religion*, 583.

[19] Calvin, *Institutes of the Christian Religion*, 630. The reader may recall the letter from Augustine to Jerome and see the similar approach.

He understood the need for what Paul called mutual encouragement.[20] Our study, with its egalitarian philosophy, finds some disagreement as he expresses the need to confess to clergy.

> Thus, although all of us ought to console one another and confirm one another in assurance of divine mercy, we see that the ministers themselves have been ordained witnesses and sponsors of it to assure our consciences of forgiveness of sins, to the extent that they are said to forgive sins and loose souls.[21]

In this project, we argue for disciple making among fellow disciples. Indeed, while we disagree with Calvin on this point, he is extremely helpful as he reflects on relations with others.

> Let us, then, unremittingly examining our faults, call ourselves back to humility. Thus, nothing will remain in us to puff us up; but there will be much location to be cast down. On the other hand, we are bidden so to esteem in regard whatever gifts of God we see in other men that we may honor those men in whom they reside. For it would be great depravity on our part to deprive them of that on her which the Lord has bestowed upon them.[22]

Calvin affirms confession among the laity, but it is very clear that, in his view, pastors "are better fitted than the others" for this counsel because of calling of the Lord. While I agree that pastors have, presumably, more training and experience to guide the faithful, Calvin goes too far. Indeed, this is too close to the clergy-laity problem discussed in Chapter Five. He does, nonetheless provide a sound theological ground for what we are calling disciple making by fellow disciples. With this glimpse of these two reformers, we see that they were disciple makers. In the decades following the reformers, the movement became established and, as some would call it, stale. It was in response to this shift that another movement sprang from the Reformation. This new movement was, in the assessment of some, a second phase of the Reformation, Pietism.

---

[20] Cf. Romans 1:12.

[21] Calvin, *Institutes of the Christian Religion*, 636.

[22] Calvin, *Institutes of the Christian Religion*, 634.

Applicative Questions

Like others before them we see the reformers using the writing of letters to communicate with fellow disciples. When was the last time you put pen to paper to encourage a friend in his or her walk with the Lord? Imagine the surprise for a friend to receive a brief note from you in which they are encouraged to press on in their personal spiritual development. Why not take a moment and write such a note right now?

Calvin urged confession, to whom on earth do you go in obedience to James admonishment, to confess your sins?

CHAPTER TEN

EXPLORING DISCIPLE MAKING SINCE THE REFORMATION

The Pendulum Swings from Protestant Scholasticism

Regardless of the life-giving work of the early Reformers, in the era following the reformation, there grew a theological coldness, a dryness within many Protestant churches. Pietism emerged in response to this weakened condition within Protestantism. Pietists sought to call the church back to a life of following God. There was a moral laxity that, said the Pietists, was a direct result of preaching that had become so theological as to be ineffectual in the lives of its hearers. F. Ernest Stoeffler, one of the key thinkers on the subject, describes the reaction of August Francke (1663-1727), who decries the situation in Germany in the late 17th century. Franke asserted that people simply went to church for confession and communion four times a year. This religious activity had no effect on their way of life.[1] The Pietist reaction to this inert Christianity was "what they called an 'active' (*tätig*) approach."[2] As such, Stoeffler characterizes Pietism as "oppositive"[3] and was the natural outgrowth of the Reformation and its principles of living.[4] This reaction was against what some, including Christopher Barnett describes as "Protestant Scholasticism."[5] This form of Scholasticism created a situation where pastors had placed the pursuit of theology at such a high level that they did not provided pastoral care for their congregations. They would purport theological hypotheticals in their pulpits in such a manner that hearers did not understand. In reaction to this, leaders would emerge to call their congregations to renewal by focusing on their personal discipleship.

---

[1] F. Ernest Stoeffler, *German Pietism During the Eighteenth Century* (Leiden, Netherlands: E. J. Brill, 1973), 21.

[2] Stoeffler, *German Pietism*, 21.

[3] F. Ernest Stoeffler, *The Rise of Evangelical Pietism* (Leiden, Netherlands: E.J. Brill, 1971), 22.

[4] Stoeffler, *The Rise of Evangelical Pietism*, 23.

[5] Christopher Barnett, *Kierkegaard, Pietism and Holiness* (New York: Routledge, 2011), 8.

Because of the emphasis on pious living that may be called personal discipleship, Pietism is a movement important for our consideration in this exploration if disciple making. Among the more significant figures is Jacob Spener (1635-1705), a 17th century German Lutheran pastor.

Spener: Seeking Balance Between Theology and Practice

In Pietism, the pendulum is swinging from, what some might call dry, theological pursuit, to a life-giving model of personal discipleship. Spener's work reacts against a dry theological Protestantism that contains "so much wood, hay, and stubble of human inquisitiveness that gold can no longer be seen."[6] Central to Pietist literature is Spener's *Pia Desideria*. A book that, intriguingly, is not a work of disciple making as we would describe the writings of the Desert Fathers or Augustine's *Enchiridion*, or Luther's *Simple Way to Pray*. While it does contain challenges to what we call disciple making it is really a manifesto toward the pious life. Spener calls for reform among civil authorities, church and clergy, people and their offences. He writes at length against drunkenness, lawsuits, business ethics and other topics and then about educational institutions. Indeed, to read *Pia* is to understand why Stoeffer called Pietism "oppositive." In this work, Spener also gives a list of helpful books to read for edification, many of which come from Mystical schools of thought.

The influence of Pietism would be widespread through the likes of Spener, Francke and Ludwig von Zinzendorf. Indeed, the movement was influential in theological development reaching even to Friedrich Schleiermacher and Karl Barth who asserted the importance of Pietism to 19th century Christianity.[7] For a study of disciple making, there is much to be learned from the Pietists.[8] We will focus briefly on one facet of the movement.

One of the great emphases of Pietism is the reading and the study of

---

[6] Jacob Spener, *Pia Desideria*, Theodore Tappert, trans. and ed. (Minneapolis, MN: Fortress Press, 1964), Kindle location 912.

[7] Barnett, *Kierkegaard, Pietism and Holiness*, 32.

[8] The scope of this inquiry does not allow for the kind of investigation into Pietism that the author may wish, thus the work of August Francke, Gerhard Tersteegen, Nicolas Von Zinzendorf and others, while important, must be bypassed. For further introduction into the Pietists, the reader is directed to Stoeffler, *The Rise of Evangelical Pietism*.

the Bible in the church, among individuals and by families. But there was another layer of Bible activity that is of particular significance to our study. The 'conventicle,' *ecclesiola in ecclesia* (church in a church), was a small gathering for Bible reading, study and application. In Spener's system, a clergyman would be present in the small gathering to aid the faithful. The purpose was to bring the Bible to bear on the heart and life in keeping with the aims stated in *Pia Desideria*. This process of regular attendance in very small groups could have a major influence in the growth of the faithful. A sermon might only reach the mind, or only be partially comprehended. It was in the meeting of the conventicle that understanding could move the truths of Scripture from the mind to the heart and then out into the life of the faithful. There is mystical influence on the Pietists as they were, at varying levels, seeking experience with God. This is the pendulum's swing from dry theological teaching to life-giving Bible discussion and application. Pietism, in various forms, would make its way to England, have some influence on the Wesleys, and migrate to America.

19th Century: Textual Discoveries, Criticism and Responses

The Pietists' had a lasting influence on those who sought balance between theology and practice. Simultaneous to their development as a movement, in the 18th and 19th centuries, a growing flood of ancient biblical manuscripts (MSS.) were discovered. Higher Criticism emerged from the rationalism of the day and had a significant impact on theological scholarship. This is true on each end of the theological spectrum. There was renewed interest in the original meaning of the biblical writers as well as history of the interpretation. Their endeavor was to understand the original use and meaning of biblical texts, especially with an ever-growing supply of older manuscripts to study. This proves valuable to our quest for better understanding of our key word in Matthew.

Baptist scholars of the mid-nineteenth century were among those who were engaged in study of the text in its original language. They were, like others on both sides of the Atlantic, taking advantage of the discovery of newly available MSS. John Broadus was a preeminent mid-19th century scholar in America. Commenting on Matthew 28:19, he states that to make a disciple is "to bring him into the relation of pupil to teacher."[9] We may infer

---

[9] John A. Broadus, *Commentary on Matthew*, (Grand Rapids, MI.:

two steps: a) evangelism to bring one into the relationship, and b) the importance of the relationship. In the case of biblical disciple making the 'teacher' that Broadus refers to is not a mere human. He asserts that our teacher is, in fact, Jesus, "the Great Teacher"[10] who "has perfect wisdom and unlimited authority."[11] In this, he makes an important contribution to our discussion on disciple making. As fellow disciples, we bring one another to our Master and Authority, Jesus. Following Broadus, we see the idea of fellow disciples walking together behind the Savior. Isn't this Paul's hope of mutual encouragement in Romans 1:12? Don't we see this clearly in the letter to the Philippians? Isn't this a recurring theme as Jesus taught His disciples about servant leadership (Matthew 20) and not being called Rabbi or instructor (Matthew 23)? While a more experienced disciple may, certainly, shed light on Scripture and life for another who is less experienced, the emphasis must remain on pointing one another to Jesus as our only master.

Recent Scholarship

Since the last quarter of the 20th century, there is no uniform opinion regarding how to interpret the Matthean Great Commission. We undertook a survey of over 100 commentaries from across the theological spectrum from the 19th and 20th centuries. Some scholars advocate proclamation, others say little at all about the matter while interpreting the two uses of (the English or Latin) 'teach' simply as a command to preach the gospel (which is, of course, a laudable, though truncated point of view). But as time has passed there has emerged an understanding about the original meaning and intent of the text within its original context as we see in France, Luz and others in Chapter Two. In recent scholarship, the prevailing understanding is that μαθητεύσατε (*mathēteusate*) should be understood to mean 'make disciples.'

William Hendriksen, a scholar-pastor who was among the first writers published by Baker Book House, posed an important question: "what is meant by 'make disciples'?"[12] He asserts that Jesus does not mean "make

---

Kregel Publications, 1990), 593.

    [10] Broadus, *Commentary on Matthew*, 593.
    [11] Broadus, *Commentary on Matthew*, 593.
    [12] William Hendriksen, *Exposition of the Gospel According to Matthew*. New Testament Commentary (Grand Rapids, MI: Baker Book House, 1973), 999.

converts."[13] Instead, as we have seen earlier, the accurate translation is to make ongoing, lifelong students of Jesus. It is also noteworthy that Hendricksen draws a distinction between the mind, the heart and the volition, saying that our "term 'make disciples' places more stress on the fact that the mind, as well as the heart and the will, must be won for God."[14] He focuses on the student/pupil aspect while asserting a holistic view. "True *discipleship* implies much more. Mere mental understanding does not as yet make one a disciple." The teaching of Jesus must become part of the "heart, mind, and will, so that one *remains* or *abides* in the truth. Only then is one truly Christ's 'disciple'" (John 8:31).[15] Indeed this emphasis on the heart, mind and will are congruent with the widely relied upon teaching of Dallas Willard. He states that our view of life and our circumstances depend on "what we have become in the depths of our being—in our spirit, will, or heart."[16] Taking a cue from Hendrickson and Willard (like the Pietists before them) we argue that what Jesus meant by μαθητεύσατε (*mathēteusate*/make disciples) is fellow disciples urging one another on in an ever-changing life, guided by the heart and mind as students of the Master. New Testament scholar Francis Wright Beare states that for one to be a disciple requires "the willingness to be a servant to all, the commitment to do the will of the heavenly Father."[17] This echoes France, that discipleship "is not complete unless it leads them to a life of observing Jesus' Commandments."[18] Thus the question follows: Which commands?

What Jesus means when He tells us to obey all that he commanded is interpreted in numerous ways. For New Testament scholar Rudolf Schnackenburg, Matthew had already made his understanding of disciple making clear, "especially The Sermon on the Mount (see 5:1), the discourse to the disciples in chapter 10, and the discourse on the community (see 18:1);..."[19] Schnackenberg's summary is helpful but does not mention

---

[13] Hendriksen, *Gospel According to Matthew*, 999.

[14] Hendriksen, *Gospel According to Matthew*, 999.

[15] Hendriksen, *Gospel According to Matthew*, 999.

[16] Willard, *Renovation*, 13.

[17] Francis Wright Beare, *The Gospel According to Matthew: A Commentary* (Oxford: Blackwell, 1981), 545.

[18] R. T. France, *Matthew*, vol. 1, Tyndale New Testament Commentaries (Grand Rapids, MI: Eerdmans Publishing, 1985), 415.

[19] Rudolf Schnackenburg, *The Gospel of Matthew*. Robert R. Barr, trans. (Grand Rapids, MI: Eerdmans, 2002), 298-299.

essentials such as the 'Greatest Commandment'[20] to love God first and neighbors second as well as the 'New Commandment' to love one another.[21] Life together in community, walking together behind Jesus, discussing, applying and obeying His teachings in concrete and personal ways. This is a theological and practical understanding of what commands a disciple is obeying as a function of their personal discipleship and disciple making. Our final example of disciple making made disciples in the academy, on the military base, on the radio and through writing (even today). It is to C. S. Lewis that we turn next.

Applicative Questions

How could you adapt the Pietist 'church in a church model in your context?

Are you unbalanced: toward the theological or the experiential?

How could your congregation could adapt the idea of the conventicle?

Do you think the assertion that questions among friends in regular conversation will help us gain better understanding of the gospel and what it means to be a disciple of Jesus is too simplistic? Why or why not?

[20] Mark 12:29-31.
[21] John 13:34-35.

CHAPTER ELEVEN

C. S. LEWIS AS DISCIPLE MAKER

To begin this aspect of our quest, we remember the emphasis on friendship that was first considered in Augustine's interaction with Jerome in Chapter Eight.[1] "I admit that I can easily rest myself to their love, especially when I am worn out by the scandals of this world and I can rest in their love, free from cares and convinced that God is there."[2] With Augustine's words in mind, we assert that friendship is not just a fruit of disciple making, but a key to it. We recall the assertion of Jacobitz. "For Augustine, friends are companions who, insofar as they rest in God, speak the truth with authority. A friend might even be the better judge of one's own character than one's self."[3] From Augustine we see the importance of cultivating friendships that God uses to bring us closer to Him. To borrow from Jacobitz, friends can see us better than we might see ourselves. To deepen our exploration of this concept, we turn to the writing of one of the most influential figures of the Twentieth Century.

The Significance of C. S. Lewis

Is there a more significant figure in twentieth century Christianity than C. S. Lewis? Through his books, broadcast talks, and essays, Lewis emerged a thinker for the common man. Not a clergyman, Lewis was a layman in the Anglican church. In his writing, he appealed to the everyday Christian as well as the pastor or scholar. Introducing a tribute to Lewis by J. I. Packer in their celebration of Lewis' 100th birthday in 1998, *Christianity Today* asserts that Lewis, for Evangelicals, was their Aesop, Augustine and

---

[1] The importance of friendship in disciple making will become clear in the explanation of the Pulpit-Table Tandem in Chapter Sixteen.

[2] Gerard Jacobitz, "The Epistolary Correspondence of Saints Jerome and Augustine and the Expansion of the Rule of Saint Benedict from 66 to 73 Chapters" in *American Benedictine Review*, Vol. 63, Issue 4 (Dec 2012), 392.

[3] Jacobitz, "Correspondence of Saints Jerome and Augustine," 403.

Aquinas.[4] *The Chronicles of Narnia, Surprised by Joy,* and *Mere Christianity* come to mind, illustrating perhaps, the storytelling, confession and the theology aspects that cause him to deserve such an accolade. There is little debate about the influence of C. S. Lewis on the thinking of greater Evangelicalism. Indeed, an exhaustive exploration of his work in the context of discipleship would fill its own book. In this work, we contend that his writing shaped the discipleship of his readers and in his life, he shaped and was shaped in discipleship with his friends.

Discipled into Belief?

First, though, I include a personal anecdote for context. In a meeting in Sarajevo with colleagues, I was being briefed on an important gospel movement in missions. This movement was referred to as, aptly enough, a Disciple Making Movement. In this explanation about disciples making disciples, there was something that had not previously occurred to me. The idea was that people can be discipled *into* belief. As the discussion continued, I realized that I had been *discipled into belief* some thirty years earlier. I had not responded to an 'altar call' in an evangelistic service. I had, rather, through conversation with a mentor and study of the Bible with him, come to understand that the Bible made sense and the claims in it about Jesus were true. With that understanding, I realized that I was in trouble because of my sin and that I had never believed in the God of forgiveness. That evening, I prayed my first real prayer. In what follows, we will examine how Lewis was, arguably, discipled into belief, grew in discipleship and then practiced disciple-making.

Much has been written about the 'conversion' of C. S. Lewis. This process was influenced by none other than Lewis' friend, J. R. R. Tolkien. Lewis and Tolkien, colleagues at Oxford, had engaged in many conversations about writing, myths, languages and about Christianity. In an October 18, 1931 letter to his longtime friend Arthur Greeves, Lewis describes a momentous conversation.

Now what Dyson and Tolkien showed me was this: that if I met the

---

[4] J. I. Packer, "Still Surprised by Lewis" in *Christianity Today*, vol. 42, no. 10 (September 7, 1998). http://www.christianitytoday.com/ct/1998/september7/8ta054.html (accessed 3/4/17).

idea of sacrifice in a Pagan story I didn't mind at all: again, that if I met the idea of a god sacrificing himself to himself I liked it very much and was mysteriously moved by it: again, that the idea of the dying and reviving god (Balder, Adonis, Bacchus) similarly moved me provided I met it anywhere *except* in the Gospels.[5]

It was an extended conversation about myth that brought Lewis to an understanding of the significance of imagination in understanding God. British scholar Alister McGrath clarifies that Tolkien fostered Lewis' understanding that the challenge was not in "rational failure" as much as in "imaginative failure"[6] and that Lewis had no trouble with the idea of myth. Tolkien was trying to show Lewis that myth had a basis in truth. It was because of the hours of previous conversations that Lewis made the step toward becoming a Christian that night. We assert that through these conversations, Lewis had become the pupil. As conversations continued, Lewis ascended to belief. As he states to Greeves in the same letter: "Now the story of Christ is simply a true myth: a myth working on us in the same way as the others, but with this tremendous difference that it *really happened*: ... I am almost *nearly* certain that it really happened."[7] Lewis' friends, Tolkien and Hugo Dyson, invested in him and heard his arguments. In those long conversations, they aided him in arriving at a place of near certitude about Jesus. While this is a fascinating topic for deeper exploration, this is not the place for more about Lewis' journey to belief.[8] Perhaps the lesson for us today is that we should engage less via computer and smartphone screens and engage more face to face with friends who may be or may become fellow disciples. We should walk with friends as fellow learners, so that they may

---

[5] C. S. Lewis, *The Collected Letters of C. S. Lewis, Vol. I: Family Letters 1905-1931, ed.* Walter Hooper (New York: HarperSanFrancisco, 2004), 976-7.

[6] Alister McGrath, *C. S. Lewis – A Life: Eccentric Genius, Reluctant Prophet* (Carol Stream: Tyndale House Publishers, 2013), 149.

[7] C. S. Lewis, *The Collected Letters, Vol. I*, 977.

[8] For an excellent investigation of the details surrounding the conversion of Lewis, one should begin with C. S. Lewis, *Surprised by Joy*. The work of Alister McGrath, which analyzes the conversion, and its dating, from all available writings, is further enlightening. McGrath considers the writings and biographies and suggests an alternate view on the sequence of events. See Chapter 6, "The Most Reluctant Convert: The Making of a Mere Christian" in *C. S. Lewis - A Life: Eccentric Genius, Reluctant Prophet.*

believe in our Master and truly follow Him.

Lewis on Friendship

We assert that friendship is a key to disciple making. We have just seen how important conversations between friends are in Lewis' journey. Let's look at his own words about friendship. His understanding was not at all limited to a Christian context but was informed by a deep knowledge of language and history. For Lewis, to have friends meant to meet regularly. It is in these gatherings that the importance of the group comes to light. Consider this description from his essay "Friendship."

> By myself I am not large enough to call the whole man into activity; I want other lights than my own to show all his facets. Now that Charles is dead, I shall never again see Ronald's reaction to a specifically Caroline joke. Far from having more of Ronald, having him "to myself" now that Charles is away, I have less of Ronald. Hence true Friendship is the least jealous of loves. Two friends delight to be joined by a third, and three by a fourth, if only the newcomer is qualified to become a real friend. They can then say, as the blessed soul say in Dante, "here comes one who will augment our loves." For in this love "to divide is not to take away."[9]

From this we may take several helpful points. In established friendships, we know one another well enough to help each other see truth about ourselves, to see *our* own 'whole' person. My friends who know me well can help me see my flaws better than I can alone. Secondly, to add to a group of friends for conversation does not divide attention as cutting a pie into eight slices renders smaller portions than six. Adding friends to a group 'augments' perspectives (borrowing from the quote). This is because the additional perspectives foster understanding. Thus, the Caroline joke reference. In the context of disciple making, these broader perspectives help us grow as disciples. Before moving forward, we should glean some insight from Lewis about some beginning bases for friendship.

---

[9] C. S. Lewis "Friendship" in *Four Loves* (London: Bles, 1960 repr., New York: Inspirational Press, 1987), 246.

We noted earlier that Lewis and Tolkien shared many topics of conversation aside from Christianity. There are various bases for friendship as Lewis states.

> For us of course the shared activity and therefore the companionship on which Friendship supervenes will not often be a bodily one like hunting or fighting. It may be a common religion, common studies, a common profession, even a common recreation. All who share it will be our companions; but one or two or three who share something more will be our Friends.[10]

This is directly applicable to our assertion that the larger gathering of the local congregation will not suffice alone in disciple making. Sitting with us in our congregation, most share a common belief, but to be fellow disciples on a journey, means to, as friends, "share something more."[11] This sharing could be based in a hobby, a sport or our profession. This leads to an important question. What was the role of groups, such as the now famous Inklings, in Lewis' growth as a disciple?

The Ongoing Influence of Friends

His earliest work of apologetics was *The Problem of Pain* (1940). In his biography of Lewis, longtime friend and former student George Sayer (1914-2005) describes the influence of Lewis' peers on the book noting that Lewis "read chapters to the Inklings before the book was published and dedicated it to Havard and Tolkien, who had provided many suggestions.[12] There is no doubt that the Inklings were influential in the writings of their members. The group met weekly for years on various days, at various times and in several places. The most well-known, perhaps, being at 11:00 am on Tuesdays at the Eagle and Child pub. In these meetings, they read their writings aloud for criticism and collaboration. It is noteworthy that physician, Dr. Robert E. Havard and Tolkien had a significant part in the development of the work. The hard subject of pain and suffering is among the best fodder for disciple

---

[10] C. S. Lewis, "Friendship," 248.

[11] C. S. Lewis, "Friendship," 248.

[12] George Sayer, *Jack: A Life of C. S. Lewis* (Wheaton IL: Crossway, 1988), 250.

making conversations. Sayer notes that the book was written in "plain, everyday language."[13] This is because that Lewis believed that philosophy and theology are best understood when it was presented as such. In those conversations where Lewis, Havard, and Tolkien discussed the chapters of this book in process, disciple making occurred. Soon thereafter, Lewis would articulate these lessons to the British public.

Mere Christianity

As World War II had its impact on Britain, Lewis was sought out by the BBC to give several talks on the radio. Those talks were well received and published as small volumes and eventually became *Mere Christianity*, perhaps his most widely known work. This volume is a thought-provoking tool for disciple making. It takes the reader from an argument for the existence of God, and then Jesus, through some basic theological topics, and then discusses Christian behavior. The outline of which lines up nicely with the disciple making method of Jesus as described by A. B. Bruce in Chapter Three. One would do well to introduce *Mere Christianity* as a first handbook for the life and thought of a disciple. From it we consider three statements about one's life as a disciple: training one's faith, dealing with distraction, and the importance of Christian community.

Lewis taught that we must live disciplined lives. In his discussion about *training* one's faith, he states: "That is why daily prayers and religious readings and churchgoing are necessary parts of the Christian life. We have to be continually reminded of what we believe. Neither this belief nor any other will automatically remain alive in the mind. It must be fed.[14] The mind must be constantly nurtured. He understands the difficulty of maintaining discipline. In a discussion of giving up our whole self to Christ, he advises the reader on how to deal with the vast distractions one faces, even at the beginning of each day. He urges that "the first job each morning consists simply in shoving them all back; in listening to that other voice, taking that other point of view, letting that other larger, stronger, quieter life come flowing in.[15] Lewis understood the nature of the struggle and knew it could

---

[13] Sayer, *Jack: A Life of C. S. Lewis*, 251.
[14] Lewis, *Mere Christianity*, 141.
[15] Lewis, *Mere Christianity*, 198.

not be done alone. It is in beginning the day with God in His word that our compass is reset to true north. From that filling, he reached out to others.

Learning from the Letters

As listeners heard these talks, their letters demonstrate, the impact of his words was significant. The letters he received, and answered, are a fraction of the significant disciple making words that Lewis spoke as the war continued via his broadcast talks on the BBC, preaching to the RAF, and writing letters, not to mention the lectures and sermons given in colleges, chapels and churches. But the unexpected individual fruits of the radio talks are the letters. Sayer describes that many people asked the BBC for more, but Lewis declined. He felt that he had no more to add, and that he could not keep up with even more letters.[16] But though he gave no more broadcast talks, the teaching continued. Lewis wrote to Greeves on Dec 23, 1941: "In the third place as to the aftermath of those Broadcast Talks I gave early last summer I had an enormous pile of letters from strangers to answer…"[17] Lewis took these requests for clarification and advice seriously, as he told Greeves that many of the letters were "… from serious inquirers whom it was a duty to answer fully."[18] Letter writing was a regular part of his day thereafter. These letters were not just about ideas, like Luther before him, Lewis wrote about life.

Not Just Ideas, but Life

These letters are the readiest examples of his engagement in disciple making with friends and readers. They provide not just fascinating theological discussions but, like Dr. Luther, answers to questions about everyday life and growing closer to God. One of the things we may learn from them is that Lewis did not give the impression of a know-it-all. His letters demonstrate humility as he answered questions about many subjects such as prayer, reading, and what to do if one's church is unsatisfactory. To see the value of

---

[16] Sayer, *Jack,* 260.

[17] C. S. Lewis, *The Collected Letters of C. S. Lewis, Vol. II: Books, Broadcasts, and the War 1931-1949,* Walter Hooper, ed. (New York: HarperSanFrancisco, 2004), 504.

[18] Lewis, *The Collected Letters, Vol. II,* 504.

letter writing in disciple making, we will look at a letter is to a reader, a Miss Bodle, who writes to ask about prayer, Lewis replies,

3/1/48

Dear Miss Bodle -

I v. much doubt if I'm good enough at prayer myself to advise others. First thing in the morning and last thing at night are good times but I don't find that they are the best times for one's main prayer. I prefer sometime in the early evening, before one has got sleepy - but of course it depends on how your day is mapped out.

'Grudging' tho' a nuisance need not depress us too much. It is the act of *will* (perhaps strongest where there is some disinclination to contend against) that God values, rather than the state of our emotions - the act being what we give Him, the emotions what He gives us (usually, I think, indirectly thro' the state of our body, health etc., tho' there are direct kindlings from Him too. There are *presents*, to be given thanks for but never counted on).

Of course it is very difficult to keep God only before one for more than a few seconds. Our minds are in ruins before we bring them to Him & the rebuilding is gradual. It may help to *practice* concentration on other objects twice a week quite apart from ones [sic] prayer: i.e. sit down looking at some physical object (say, a flower) and try for a few minutes to attend exclusively to it, *quietly* (never impatiently) rejecting the train of thought & imagination wh. keep starting up. All good wishes.

Yours sincerely
C. S. Lewis[19]

One can see that, though he may have not felt himself expert enough on the subject, Lewis was willing to share his own experience with his correspondent. He recognizes that discipline is hard, but needed. As he had said earlier in one of the radio broadcasts, we must train our faith.[20] While these urgings come from a distance, they are just the kind of conversation that fellow disciples might have over coffee or at a meal. Further, we may

---

[19] Lewis, *The Collected Letters, Vol. II*, 826.
[20] Cf. Lewis, *Mere Christianity*, 139-140.

understand that while face to face disciple making is certainly preferable, communicating via letter on a personal level is indeed helpful to the task.

Lewis on Community

We will propose in Chapter Eight that congregations should supplement the work in their large gatherings by fostering friendships and regular, honest and vulnerable conversations. Lewis speaks of the body of Christ as a community. In an address originally given to the ecumenical Society of St. Albans and St. Sergius and later published as "Membership" in *The Weight of Glory*, he states: "The society into which the Christian is called at baptism is not a collective but a Body. It is in fact that Body of which the family is an image on the natural level."[21] In this context ten men using shovels to dig a ditch are a collective. Whereas a family is a group of people using different abilities toward an objective. This is like the Pauline injunction in Ephesians 4 of different offices, or 1 Corinthians 12 as he lists the different gifts. Paul was fond of relating the body of Christ to a body with different organs who are interdependent upon one another. The body of Christ is the Church which exists to bring God glory. Later in the same essay Lewis clarifies. "In this way then, the Christian Life defends the single personality from the collective, not by isolating him but by giving him the status of an organ in the mystical body."[22] In community, friends remind one another of their individual value while being honest about their flaws, and the ways that they may deepen their communion with God and thus the body of Christ. We are warned at the beginning of each airplane flight to put the oxygen mask on yourself before aiding others. Thus, one must care first for one's self before caring for others. Because it is *personal* discipleship, I will turn to the first person narrative as I share some of my own story as illustration.

---

[21] C. S. Lewis, "Membership" in *The Weight of Glory* (New York: MacMillan, 1949; repr., Grand Rapids, MI: William B. Eerdmans, 1979), 35.
[22] Lewis, *The Weight of Glory*, 38-39.

Applicative Questions

Luther and Lewis, like Antony, Augustine and Aquinas before them were available to people, if not in person, by letter. Are you accessible? Do people feel free to approach you or reach out to you for guidance? What are ways that you need to become more available to those disciples you may help guide?

Think of the experience of walking together with a friend as he or she discovered the reality of the gospel. With whom could you embark on such a journey now?

Was the idea of being discipled into belief a new idea to you? Who, in your circle could you invite into regular conversation about Scripture in life? They might be the next C. S. Lewis.

PART THREE

BEING AND MAKING

CHAPTER TWELVE

PERSONAL DISCIPLESHIP: THROUGH DISCIPLINE TO DEPTH

Thus far, our exploration has included narratives that depict a variety of disciple making methods and ideas from Jesus and the lives of figures in Christian history. Informed by those ideas and models, our inquiry now considers two final and practical questions: First, how does one facilitate one's personal discipleship? Secondly, how can one obey Jesus and make disciples? It is helpful to consider the questions in the given order. In this chapter, we will consider practical ideas about the first question and in the next chapter, the second question.

To pursue one's own spiritual development is foundational to employing disciple making methods with fellow disciples. The first question (How does one facilitate one's own discipleship?) *should not* be viewed as a prerequisite for gathering with fellow disciples. In that gathering, we extend grace, exhortation and encouragement to urge one another on. We may find that God uses other disciples to motivate us to enliven our own personal discipleship. Ultimately that motivation should be understood simply in terms of loving God.

Our Motivation: Loving God

We should point one another to His love. It is very important, before we have gone too far in this section of our study, to clarify our proper motivation. Love. Appropriately enough, it is a scribe who asks Jesus about the commandments. "Jesus answered, 'The most important is, 'Hear, O Israel: The Lord our God, the Lord is one. And you shall love the Lord your God with all your heart and with all your soul and with all your mind and with all your strength.'"[1]

When a scribe asks about the Law, he is essentially asking, for him, the most important question. Jesus' answer is to *love God*. He was, of course quoting the Law. He states that our first priority as His disciples is to love the

---

[1] Mark 12:29.

Lord with all of our being: heart, soul, mind and strength. Our aim is singular, to love God with all we have. From this love will spring all the rest. But our motivation should be the expression of love for God. This is not to say that what we describe is easy. But it is to say that we need to discipline ourselves to cultivate this love. This requires a decision to love.

Our motivation in the disciplines should not be to develop the tools to do great things, though by God's sovereignty, that may be a result. Nor should our motivation be to become more spiritual in and of itself, for that will, very likely, lead to spiritual pride or self-righteousness. Our motivation should be our love for God and its increase. Our love for God should be such that our love for Him evokes a desire to do the things necessary to grow in Him. This is where we may see obedience. If one does not awake each morning looking forward to the time that is set aside to be alone with the Father, then gaining that kind of discipline should be first on our list of prayer requests. When we realize that there is nothing in a human relationship that can compare to the joy possible in our relationship with God, we will change the way we approach Him. This joy is not a passing emotion; it is a lasting recognition of the presence and grace of God that is with us no matter what. What follow are some practices that facilitate this love of God. Love is learned. When we cultivate our love of God, we approach our practices with anticipation, not drudgery. I am not advocating becoming a hermit, the whole point is to follow the greatest and next commandments, loving God *and neighbor*. Time with God make that neighbor relationship better.

There will be fruit from this union of the whole self with God, restoration. Dallas Willard explains that this restoration (one may think of Romans 5) is the "ideal of the spiritual life."[2] From our own restoration with Him and reliance on Him, a fruit of this communion with God will be better relationships with the humans in our world. But, fruit comes from cultivation. We cultivate through discipline. Paul tells us to "pray without ceasing."[3] To awake each day anticipating our personal conversation with God, and then to joyfully speak with Him throughout the day, and finally, to close one's eyes at night praying one's self to sleep, these can be the ongoing joys of approaching the discipline of loving God. Personal history tells me that this will not be our experience every day. But, getting to the delight with God is worth the

---

[2] Dallas Willard, *Renovation of the Heart* (Colorado Springs, CO: NavPress, 2002), 30.

[3] 1 Thessalonians 5:17.

diligent discipline necessary, and which we will consider next.

Personal Discipleship

We assert in Chapter Two that the word discipleship is ubiquitous and ambiguous. To avoid confusion, let's make clear what we mean by personal discipleship. We just considered the importance of loving God as proper motivation. In a particularly hard saying in the minds of some, Jesus proclaims:

> Not everyone who says to me, 'Lord, Lord,' will enter the kingdom of heaven, but the one who does the will of my Father who is in heaven. On that day many will say to me, 'Lord, Lord, did we not prophesy in your name, and cast out demons in your name, and do many mighty works in your name?' And then will I declare to them, 'I never knew you; depart from me, you workers of lawlessness.'[4]

The crowds, as Matthew puts it, were "astonished at his teaching."[5] If one carefully considers these words of Jesus, one may see the motivation behind this project. Many who sit in churches week in and week out may be shocked to hear words like these. That is because they have, likely, been presented with a kind of condensed Christianity, one that is void of hard teachings. In my plea for personal discipleship, the hope is that all who call on, and trust in the name of Jesus will practice personal discipleship. If we are redeemed by the work of Christ, then we, as an outgrowth of our love for Him, should be engaged in personal discipleship.

Secondly, personal discipleship is defined here as a disciplined life of growth in the "grace and knowledge of our Lord Jesus Christ."[6] The proof of this development is manifested when ongoing fruit develops and continues to grow. Every disciple begins from and grows to a different place than all others. In *Mere Christianity*, Lewis contrasts the fictional characters 'Christian Miss Bates' and 'Dick Firkin.' The former had a tough background before Christ. The later never became a Christian. Lewis points out that the niceness

---

[4] Matthew 7:21-23.
[5] Matthew 7:28.
[6] 2 Peter 3:18.

of Dick Firkin is a result of his background. Miss Bates' general unkindness is better than it was before Christ, but still worse than nice Dick Firkin. One's growth in spiritual fruit is individual and should be measured against where he or she was, not compared to other people. A great danger in our congregations today is that they are filled with nice people, not new men.[7] As one makes time every day to commune with God, an ongoing fruit-bearing life develops. Consider Robert Coleman's description. "Facilitating the learning process was discipline, a quality inherent in discipleship. In fact, both words are derived from the same root. Sincere disciples of Christ accept His rules of conduct, as in a school, bringing every thought into obedience to their Master."[8] To be clear, this fruit is not a result of one's labor as diet and exercise can improve one's annual cholesterol report. This fruit is the result of the disciple intentionally connecting him or herself daily to God who then works in and through them. As we look at Jesus' words about the vine and the branches (John 15) and Paul's words about the fruit of the Spirit (Galatians 5:22-23), we see that the fruit is God working *in us*, not our own achievement. Personal discipleship is about putting oneself into the hands of God daily so that God may work in and through him or her. In what follows we will consider the various means that facilitate this personal discipleship, what many refer to as spiritual development.

Spiritual Development

Spiritual development is a broadly used term. The word 'spiritual' may invite confusion or concern about meaning, especially in pluralistic contexts. It is a problematic term for some, perhaps because of a negative association. In a conversation with my college history professor about Christ, he told me that he didn't want to be a Christian, but that he considered himself spiritual. C. S. Lewis, ever the stickler for right definition, states that we should

---

[7] Cf. "Nice People or New Men" in C. S. Lewis, *Mere Christianity*, (New York: Macmillan, 1952; repr, New York, HarperCollins, 2009) Kindle., 210ff.
    [8] Robert E. Coleman, *The Master Plan of Discipleship* (Old Tappan, NJ: Fleming H. Revell, 1987), p. 100.

be aware of the ambiguity in the word *spiritual*. There are many New Testament contexts in which it means "pertaining to the (Holy) Spirit," and in such contexts the spiritual is, by definition, good. But when *spiritual* is used simply as the opposite of corporeal, or instinctive, or animal, this is not so.[9]

Lewis brings Scripture to bear in a helpful manner. We seek above all to be biblical and clear in the use of terms. To alleviate any confusion or concern about the concept of spiritual development a definition is needed. Christian spiritual development, like personal discipleship, is the activity that one undertakes to "grow in the grace and knowledge of our Lord Jesus Christ."[10] This leads us to the question. 'How?' And 'what is the activity?' Over the centuries this activity has been referred to as the Christian disciplines. These disciplines have seen a resurgence in interest in recent years.

Christian Disciplines

The Christian disciplines are steps that we may take or habits we form to grow in our knowledge of and relationship with God. The disciplines should not be pursued for their own sake, or even to make us a better person. The purpose of a discipline is to move us closer to communion with God. *He develops* us as we move toward Him. I have often tried to relate it to climbing onto a table where a surgery is performed. In the analogy, God is the surgeon who is working on my heart and mind, my role is simply to put myself in place and to open myself to His work. This is the purpose of the disciplines.

There is no more recognized name today, among evangelicals, regarding the disciplines than Richard Foster. Foster wrote the, now classic, *Celebration of Discipline: The Path to Spiritual Growth*[11] in 1978. His work, along with those of Thomas Merton, Dallas Willard, Henri Nouwen, and others, has helped many to see the value of the disciplines. His book is widely used as a handbook for employing disciplines to spiritual development. As *Mere Christianity* provides a primer for simple apologetics, doctrine and life,

---

[9] C. S. Lewis "Friendship" in *Four Loves* (London: Bles, 1960 repr., New York: Inspirational Press, 1987), 244-5.

[10] 2 Peter 3:18.

[11] Richard Foster, *Celebration of Discipline* (New York, HarperCollins, 1978).

Celebration of Discipline does the same for the disciplined life of the disciple. Foster's mentor, Dallas Willard, cautions us, however, that "...we need not try to come up with a complete list of disciplines. Nor should we assume that our list will be right for others."[12] This might remind the reader of Lewis' counsel to Miss Bodle in Chapter Six in which he noted that every person must find their own best system for prayer. Thomas à Kempis concurs. "All people cannot have the same disciplines, but this is more proper for one, that for another."[13] Each of us is different and must find our own way of devotion. What follows is not a checklist as much as it is a menu. But there are some selections that really are essential to a well-balanced diet. With that we take a brief look at different disciplines.

Applicative questions

How regular are your own spiritual disciplines? Daily? Three times a week? Imagine you received the following email.

> Dear _____, After many years of sitting in church 2.7 Sundays a month, I have decided to really become a student of Jesus. But I'm puzzled by what I need to do in my 'quiet time' that people talk about. Would you describe your own daily practice so I can understand what to do?

Sit for a moment and write a reply to this request explaining what, how and why you do practice your personal spiritual discipline.

---

[12] Dallas Willard, *Spirit of the Disciplines* (New York: HarperCollins, 1988), 156-157.

[13] Thomas à Kempis, *The Imitation of Christ*, trans. William Creasy (Notre Dame, IN: Ave Maria Press, 1989), 48.

CHAPTER THIRTEEN

PRACTICING THE DISCIPLINES DAILY

Among the recognized thinkers on the subject, Richard Foster lists meditation, prayer, fasting, study, simplicity, solitude, submission, service, confession, worship, guidance, and celebration.[1] In *Spirit of the Disciplines,* Dallas Willard catalogs solitude, silence, fasting, frugality, chastity, secrecy, sacrifice, study, worship, celebration, service, prayer, fellowship, confession, and submission[2] While not a work on disciplines *per se,* in his seminal work, *Prayer: Experiencing Awe and Intimacy with God,* Timothy Keller differentiates between Bible Study, Bible reading and Bible meditation.[3] Indeed, while a very different kind of book, Keller's *Prayer* is certainly a book about disciplines and the use of the Bible and prayer for spiritual development. Without question, *Prayer* belongs on one's shelf next to *Mere Christianity.* I contrast and compare these books about disciplines to demonstrate helpful diversity of perspectives. I do not assert one is more biblical than another. However, where Willard gives the 'what' and 'why', Keller's 'how' is more practical.

Isn't the Bible Enough?

In the many volumes written on these subjects one may rightly ask, as an aged saint asked me about this very project, isn't just reading the Bible enough? Fair question. Regarding the need for the instruction on the disciplines, Foster asserts that when the Bible was written there was no need

---

[1] Richard Foster, *Celebration of Discipline,* (New York, HarperCollins, 1978), iii. Foster organizes the disciplines as follows: The Inward Disciplines: Meditation, Prayer, Fasting, Study; The Outward Disciplines: Simplicity, Solitude, Submission, Service; The Corporate Disciplines: Confession, Worship, Guidance, Celebration.

[2] Dallas Willard, *Spirit of the Disciplines* (New York: HarperCollins, 1988), 158.

[3] Timothy Keller, *Prayer: Experiencing Awe and Intimacy with God* (New York: Dutton, 2014), 88ff.

for instruction since the practice of the disciplines was generally understood.[4] We err gravely in assuming the Christian population in general knows how to approach their personal discipleship. Author and apologist G. K. Chesterton deftly states: "The Christian ideal has not been tried and found wanting. It has been found difficult; and left untried."[5] For those who *do make the effort*, practicing discipleship is hard work, but so is every other worthwhile relationship. The alternative is a stagnant, immature Christianity that produces little fruit.

Choosing and Using Disciplines

Having considered a variety of the disciplines, we now explore some more familiar ones that may then form a regimen of personal discipleship. The following is suggested with the knowledge that each student of Jesus is different and must work on his or her own system that fits their personal temperaments, life and readiness. Each of us must find our own spiritual supplements, but just as we all need basics like oxygen, water and nourishment, there are basics we simply all must practice for a healthy life. We offer these examples not as model but as illustration. Thomas à Kempis is right when he clarified that "... *this* is more proper for one, *that* for another. [emphasis mine]"[6] In the pages that follow we will consider some personal reflections that illustrate how the disciplines may be used in one's own personal discipleship, or spiritual development.

Prayer and Bible reading are core practices among Evangelicals, in their regular devotions, quiet time or whatever title they give to their time of devotion with and to God. They are, if I may, the oxygen and water referred to above. Many find that their minds are better aligned with God for prayer after investing time in Scripture. I've learned that my ability to communicate with God in prayer is enhanced following the reading of Scripture. As such, I contend that it is not enough to read occasionally or two or three times a week. There is too much in today's world to distract us from aligning our heart and mind with God. We should read daily and read in a way that the

---

[4] Foster, *Celebration of Discipline*, 3.

[5] Gilbert. K. Chesterton, *What's Wrong with the World* (New York, NY: Dodd, Mead and Co., 1910), p.48.

[6] Thomas à Kempis, *The Imitation of Christ*, trans. William Creasy (Notre Dame, IN: Ave Maria, 1989), 48.

words get to the heart. This will seem like a law to some. But I appeal to the argument made earlier about nurturing our love of God. It is not about duty, but sometimes it is through duty that we arrive at delight.[7]

The Dangers of Neglect

In conversations with Christians, I frequently discern that my companion is struggling with this or that emotion or challenge of the heart. Perhaps he is having difficulty getting along with his wife or someone in his business or ministry. Ultimately, I ask the question. "So, how is your Bible reading going these days?" That question results from my experience, over the years, that the more my friend is struggling, the more likely it is that he hasn't made (you can't *find* time) time in his busy schedule to read the Scripture. No matter our age or season of life, neglect of God's word has a negative impact on us as disciples.

Another danger is that we get involved in helpful groups that read Christian literature of varying kinds, only to wind up reading those books to the neglect of Bible reading. There are numerous reasons for this, including the assertion of some that they can't understand the Bible and find the prose of men easier to grasp. Another reason is that some simply do not have a high view of Scripture and choose Christian literature over the Bible. This is like the particular danger experienced by busy pastors who are, rightly, deep into biblical and theological research for their sermons. It is easy to push aside personal Bible reading, rationalizing that we are already studying about the Bible. I have even heard other clerical leaders say that since they are not morning people, they put off their time with the Lord in His word until evening. This could be a valid argument, except that the danger here is that once the busy day starts, their control of the day is lost and that Bible may never be never opened. I have found this is especially true for parents whose day becomes engulfed in the lives of their children. (Yes, our children - and grandchildren - can become idols that replace God.) If we are serious about personal discipleship, we must *make the time* (since we cannot find time) and the place to sit with God in His word.

I have found that location really does matter. Even as I travel to various countries, I work hard to be undistracted as I sit with God. Whether it

---

[7] From "duty to delight" is a helpful phrase in discussing discipline. Cf. Keller, *Prayer: Experiencing Awe and Intimacy with God*, 5ff.

be a cafe, a hotel coffee shop, or in a garden near where I am staying, I know the importance of relative seclusion to foster the intimate conversation with my Heavenly Father. To determine the best surrounding is important, that said, how much of His word do we really need in a day?

How Much Bible? How Often? Which Plan?

When I first became a Christian, I was told that I should read three chapters a day and five on Sunday. This would take me through the Bible every year. This type of idea helps break the Scripture into daily sections. But I must admit that this approach was seldom as successful as one might hope. It is reported that George Mueller read the Bible over 100 times from his mid-twenties until his 70th birthday.[8] This is an inspiring model.

There is a growing plethora of systems for reading the Bible and there are more being devised daily. A few years ago, I began using a plan devised in the early 19th century by Scottish pastor Robert Murray McCheyne. It is a rigorous plan that takes the reader through the Old Testament each year and the New Testament and Psalms twice a year. The reading contains four different books each day. The system has, depending on the day, usually 4, but up to 7 chapters (in the case where I may be in a section of short Psalms). Since I began using the plan, I have found the reading more and more meaningful. I was never sure why until I was having a conversation with a younger leader about Bible reading. His struggle was that so many times the Bible just seems dry and he wasn't touched by it. I asked how much he read when he did read. His response was that he read one chapter three or four times a week when he could find time. I realize that I too often don't get a lot from the first (or even second) chapter of the reading. Frequently, my heart and mind awake to the Scripture in the third or fourth chapter. In preaching, I have tried to relate this, metaphorically, to washing the dishes with a sponge. In this metaphor, the water just runs off a

---

[8] Noted by John Piper: "By his own testimony he had read the Bible 100 times by the time he was 71."
http://www.desiringgod.org/messages/george-muellers-strategy-for-showing-god. (accessed 8/29/16). Cf. Arthur T. Pierson, *George Mueller of Bristol and His Witness to A Prayer-Hearing God* (Grand Rapids, Mich.: Kregel, 1999), 248.

completely hard and dry sponge until enough water moistens the sponge that it gains absorbency. Then it holds lots of water. My heart and mind often lack absorbency. I need to abide long enough so that I will begin to actually absorb God's word. By planning to read a few chapters each morning, we give our heart and mind time to realign its focus from the world we live in to the inspired word of God we are reading. To expect our heart and mind to just shift immediately into absorbing biblical truth is an unreasonable expectation on ourselves, especially in our environment of twenty-first century distractedness.

Obstacles to (and Solutions for) Reading the Bible Daily

Another reason that I hear is that people are not able readers. Having been an educator for a while, I certainly understand that some people are better readers than others. But today, now that most people have smart phones, it is quite easy to download a very helpful app called YouVersion. In YouVersion there is a plentiful variety of Bible translations from which most may find their reading preference. Some of those translations, like my preference, the English Standard Version (ESV) have an audio feature. A couple of years ago, during a conversation about strategies to help one of my friends be more regular in his reading of Scripture, he mentioned that on YouVersion, we can *listen* to the ESV. The next morning, I turned on the audio as I read. (There are other ways to listen to the Bible such as mp3 downloads and even CDs.) Since learning this, I have listened while I read every day. Over time, I have noticed a couple of advantages.

The first positive result, since I'm reading as I listen, is that I read more slowly and carefully than if I am just reading silently. This has the advantage of slowing my heart and mind to dwell longer on the words. Secondly, I am better able to fight the urge to skip parts of the text that I might want to 'scan.' To be honest, I've not always found the details of the Tabernacle, the genealogies, or the names of tribes returning from captivity enlightening. Sometimes, I would skim or skip these sections, I might rationalize, no harm done, right? But, as I've submitted myself to this discipline of reading and listening, I discover things in the details that I would have missed if I had hurried through.

Another thing that using a plan does for me is that it gets me regularly into parts of the Bible that I might not go to if I were choosing what to read. This suggests another caution. I do not think I should be choosing *what* I read. My tendency would be to read Paul, the Synoptics and Psalms and Isaiah but I need the whole counsel of Scripture. By submitting to a whole Bible plan, I no longer controlling my own reading. I've learned that the less I'm in control of things, the better (this is true for many areas of life). There are lots of plans and lectionaries one may use in the discipline of reading. One just needs to set the time and place and follow them.

Let me make a brief comment about 'devotional' literature. While very helpful supplements, devotional materials like Oswald Chambers' classic *My Utmost for His Highest*[9] should be just that, a supplement. Would Chambers want his work read *instead* of the Bible? I think not. We have much to learn from this genre, both ancient and modern, but it should not take the place of Scripture reading.

Time and Place

I have already dealt with this topic in passing, but this point deserves further emphasis. When I was in my early thirties, I heard a preacher tell the congregation that to meet God regularly, one needs a set time and place. I scoffed. 'Maybe you,' I thought, 'but I can do my devotions anywhere, anytime.' How wrong I was. Just to clarify, God is omnipresent, this is not about getting a 'stronger signal,' it is about finding the place that you are better able to hear from Him. For years, I struggled and stumbled. Finally, in my forties, I made my mind up to sit with God and His Word every day, in the same place, at the same time. At first, it was quite inconsistent. Over time however, I saw the fruit from dwelling in Scripture each morning and the habit formed. It is no longer a duty, it is a joy. Making the decision to cultivate one's discipleship through soaking in God's word is the first step to establishing and maintaining a regimen. It is widely believed that it takes three weeks to form a habit. This habit is crucial as it provides structure and focus in an increasingly unstructured and distracted world. Begin, begin again, and keep beginning until you've formed the habit. Press on through the duty, what Lewis called the "grudging,"[10] and the delight will come.

---

[9] Oswald Chambers, *My Utmost for His Highest* (New York: Dodd, Mead and Co., 1935, repr. Westwood, NJ: Barbour and Co., 1963).
[10] Lewis, *The Collected Letters, Vol. II*, 826.

Transition to Prayer: Memorizing and Meditating on Scripture

Before moving into prayer from Bible reading, we note that first Luther and now Keller advocate a step between reading Scripture and prayer. I have found this transition helpful. Since the point of the disciplines is to bring me into a place of communion, of abiding, I want to speak to God intimately. To do that, I should use the language He provided, a *biblical* conversation. To this end I have devised a list of Scriptures.[11] I choose these texts with one thing in mind, to remind me of how great God is. The verses are read as prayers, slowly and deliberately. "O Lord, our Lord, how majestic is your name in all the earth!"[12] "Lord, you have been our dwelling place in all generations. Before the mountains were brought forth, or ever you had formed the earth and the world, from everlasting to everlasting you are God."[13] I continue to update this list of passages on a document that I can access from my smartphone or any computer, the same can be done in a paper Bible with a pencil and bookmarks. To intentionally work at memorizing a passage slows us down. This slowness is important and becomes a meditation on Scripture. I find it helpful to use texts that explicitly describe or glorify God so that eventually my focus is more on Him and less on the words. This prepares us to pray. What is being described may be called 'praying into prayer' using Scripture. I have seen this revolutionize the connection I experience as I move from dwelling in His word to the requests I will make. In preaching about this, I've often called it 'climbing into the lap of my heavenly Father.

Petitions: Praying for Circumstances

Many Christians have a prayer list. But I have learned that these prayer requests must only be a portion of our prayers. Many Evangelicals in the English-speaking world know about the ACTS plan: adoration, confession, thanksgiving, and supplication (an older word for request, praying *for* something). I was teaching this one day in class and a student asked, "Can't it be CATS?" I looked at the white-board and laughed realizing that of course

---

[11] Appendix D contains a list of texts that have proven helpful in this transition from reading to praying.

[12] Psalm 8:9.

[13] Psalm 90:1-2.

it could. Sometimes it may be better to confess first (perhaps starting with Psalm 51 and 69 as the Scripture lead in). The point is simple in this well-used device, Prayer has many facets.

In *Prayer*, Keller asserts that Paul didn't pray for improvement in the circumstances of his friends. Instead Paul prayed for them to be drawn closer to God. I looked up from my Kindle and audibly said "No." Struck by this statement, I decided to find out. Fortunately, on my shelf was D. A. Carson's *A Call to Spiritual Reformation*. In this volume is the chapter "Praying for Others" in which Carson includes excerpts from the Pauline letters that are his published prayers.[14] I read them all carefully asking: Was Keller right? (The reality is I probably wanted to prove him wrong.) At the end, I had to agree. Paul's emphasis is less about our circumstances and more about where we are in relation to God during the circumstances. Yes, we should pray for the circumstances of people! But, in that prayer, we should pray that the challenges that they and we face are used to draw them closer to our Master. This is the focus of a disciple maker's prayer.

Prayer Journaling

A few years ago, I was in a Christian bookstore in South Africa and found a book that was helpful to me in the journey of selecting and using disciplines. At the end, there, is a chapter about journaling our prayers. The writer suggested that we take a blank notebook and write our prayers as though we are writing a daily letter to God. Intrigued, I began to practice this discipline. I noticed that as I wrote out my prayers, I was slowing down and the communication was more valuable. I was less distracted. If there was an interruption, I could look at the page and see where I left the conversation. No one would ever read these prayers, they are not a document for posterity, they are to help me communicate more meaningfully with God. I don't journal as though someone may read it, rather, I lay my concerns out before God.

Reminders to Pray

Earlier, we noted Paul's admonition to pray without pause. Brother

---

[14] D. A. Carson, *A Call to Spiritual Reformation* (Grand Rapids, MI: Baker, 1992), 67ff.

Lawrence has helped many in this area. *The Practice of the Presence of God*[15] is a helpful collection of the correspondence he had with various leaders about following God. In it he guides the reader into how one may worship God all day. A tool I find helpful is to receive reminders throughout the day. On my computers, I maintain a set of reminders to pray for this or that. Several times a day, such as at 9 am I am reminded that "a soft answer" (...turns away wrath). Since I can be an overly direct person, this reminds me not to respond brusquely or with sarcasm to someone who is angry or unkind. A great opportunity to pray occurs when our phone rings and we see it is one of our less favorite people, to pray for them will change our heart toward them. If Paul meant what he said about not ceasing to pray, we do well to make a discipline of continuing in prayer. Why not use the phone in our pocket to remind us to pray? Like the bells of a monastery call the monks to one of the daily offices, your smartphone can remind you to pray.

---

[15] Brother Lawrence, *The Practice of the Presence of God,* trans. John J. Delaney (New York: Image, 1977).

Applicative Questions

Does the discipline described here seem to you more about legalism? Why or why not?

What was new to you in this chapter?

What part of your daily discipline was not mentioned?

After thinking about this chapter, how might you change your answer to the applicative question in the last chapter?

CHAPTER FOURTEEN

OCCASIONAL (LESS FREQUENT) DISCIPLINES

Self-Evaluation

Someone sent me a document attached to an email a few years back. It was a weekly checklist that a large church used for its staff. They were to fill out this checklist before the weekly staff meeting. We all need some level of accountability. I suggest one develop a periodic checklist of areas of personal/professional evaluation to share with one or two of our closest fellow disciples. They, in turn, should ask us about the struggles we are honest about. This is about you and does not need to be reciprocated. Mine goes to the Chair of my Board and my pastor. This personalized form[1] becomes a diagnostic tool for the closest of our fellow disciples and for ourselves.

Sail – Row – Drift – Sink

Diagnostic tools are important when trying to determine the treatment of people by their physician, or the repair of their automobile by their mechanic. Determining the needs of one's heart and mind is no different. In *Prayer*, Tim Keller describes the Sail – Row – Drift – Sink metaphor.[2] In this helpful metaphor, he describes the different conditions that one may find themselves in. Sailing is the best condition where not only are you feeling God's love but see others being blessed by you. Rowing is the next condition and lacks the depth of awareness of God's working in and through one's self, yet the disciple pushes forward in prayer, Bible reading and meeting with fellow disciples. Drifting is the third condition and can be imagined as being in a boat set adrift without direction or motivation. Prayer is neglected as is Bible reading. Finally, the category of sinking is found after a

---

[1] A version of this form is provided in Appendix F.

[2] Timothy Keller, *Prayer: Experiencing Awe and Intimacy with God* (New York: Dutton, 2014), *258-9*. An adaptation has been provided in Appendix E.

period of drifting when one has completely disconnected one's self from God and community. Faith, it seems was a mirage.

I find this metaphor so helpful that it is a part of the accountability checklist in Appendix E. I use it for myself as well as in disciple making conversations. I may not be sailing, but I continue to row, because I know what it feels like to drift or sink and I want no part of that. When I find myself drifting or I find that I have rowed for a longer period of time without feeling the sails fill, I know it's time to get away with God and refocus in a more intentional manner. This intentional time is both regular and occasional.

Sabbath

Why is it that while we recognize we must avoid murder, lying, idolatry and adultery, as prohibited in the Ten Commandments, yet we feel it permissible work seven days a week? The discipline of rest is important for the body, soul and spirit. Ministry leaders of all kinds must realize that Sunday is not an effective Sabbath. Mark out time, therefore, to be at rest. Sabbath includes rest, refreshment, joy and extra intentional time with God. Dan Allender's *Sabbath*[3] has been a very helpful resource for me, especially in the context of understanding the element of joy and enjoyment on my day. As previously asserted, the disciplines should be tried, tested and included in one's own regimen of personal discipleship. How we each practice Sabbath is a matter of trying and deciding what is best us. There are some facets of the Sabbath, however, that are uniform, like the amount of time.

The Jewish form is from sundown Friday until sundown Saturday. From this, though, depending on the latitude one lives on and the time of year it could be a very long Sabbath or a very short one. The system I use is to consider the segments of the day we call 'morning,' 'afternoon' and 'evening.' There should be at least three of these consecutively to give one the time to have an effective Sabbath. It could begin at evening today and go through afternoon tomorrow. Or begin when arising tomorrow and go until arising the next day. Yes, sleeping is a big part of Sabbath so in each case 'night' counts. It's about a continuous sum of time where we do not work.

Enjoyment and refreshment are big parts of Sabbath. In one's Sabbath, there should be elements of fun, things that will bring one to laughter. Laughter is such an important part of the life God created, we need

---

[3] Dan Allender, *Sabbath* (Nashville, TN: Thomas Nelson, 2009).

116

more of it. But joy is more than just fun, or that other ubiquitous word - happiness, it is about meaning. To invest some portion of time in an activity that is meaningful to you is an important facet of Sabbath. This could vary from hiking a nearby nature trail where you drink in God's creation to attending an opera where you drink in God's gift of creativity to man, and anything in between. It depends on you. There are more things to say, that's why books like Allender's exist, but our space here is limited. Your imagination and the disciplines you choose can guide you. But, a word of clarification, I am not advocating a return to the law. This, like all disciplines is for our benefit and it should be motivated by a love for God. Another guilt-inducing thing on the ever-growing list of things to do is not helpful. Communion with God, however, is not just about meeting Him once a week.

Intentional Time Away with God

We also profit deeply from intentional and extended times of communion with God. My pastor is a good example. He urges his pastoral team to take a day a month for silence, solitude and prayer. Near the end of each year I take several days for reflection, self-evaluation and planning. I do the same thing at the end of our ministry year (June 30) as I prepare to report to our board. Each January for a few years I have hosted a retreat in the mountains of northern Hungary for a few invited leaders and urged them to use the time for reflection, evaluation and planning. When we go to the mountains, I tell them ahead of time that there will be a period of silence and urge them to turn off their cell phones. This fosters our focus on God. The point being that it is very helpful to get away, focus on God, and listen for His guidance. On such a retreat, one can utilize other disciplines.

Calling No Hermits

These practical examples from my own experience are best considered as a menu from which to work out one's own set of spiritual disciplines, creating a regimen for personal discipleship. These are steps taken toward what Willard calls training the heart and mind. But one's personal discipleship, as we have stated already, is not done in isolation. Indeed, we assert that a fundamental discipline yet mentioned is the disciple making conversation. The disciple needs to be engaged in community. A preacher once said that Christianity is a personal religion, not a private one. Willard states. "Spiritual formation, good or bad, is always profoundly social. You cannot keep it to yourself."[4] With that apt admonition let's return to our key text Matthew 28:19-20 and consider an application. We may assert that God wants the development of disciples through the disciplines in each congregation. It is to this plan of God that we turn our attention in the next chapter where we will consider the role of the congregation as an incubator for disciple making conversations.

Applicative Questions

When was the last time you took a day to get away and pray?

What are your obstacles to personal discipleship?

Write out your own regimen for personal discipleship using some of the disciplines mentioned. Share this with your spouse and closest fellow disciples. Ask them to hold you accountable for the next three weeks.

With whom are you sitting on a regular basis to have honest and vulnerable conversations about your personal discipleship? If you have no one, list four people that you might discuss how to start together.

Describe what you would enjoy as a regular facet of your Sabbath.

---

[4] Dallas Willard, *Renovation of the Heart* (Colorado Springs, CO: NavPress, 2002), 182.

CHAPTER FIFTEEN

DEVELOPING CONGREGATION BASED DISCIPLE MAKING

Through the lives that we have considered in our study we observe a common thread. These notables desire to know God deeply (theological understanding) while experiencing union with God (mysticism). Lewis had no shocking encounter with God, as did Luther, but arrived at belief through conversations with friends who walked with him to understanding. Through his fiction, his apologetics and practical theology, as well as through reading the vast array of letters, we see an investment in fellow disciples by answering questions about life and theology. Lewis teaches us that discipline is hard but necessary. More recently, Foster, Willard, and Keller inform us about the Christian disciplines that help us abide in Christ. This is how He renews our minds.[1] These disciplines are steps in personal discipleship which includes our project's initial focus, disciple making.

The Motivation for disciple making

Before moving into the practical aspects of the disciple making paradigm we must be mindful of our motivation. In Chapter Seven, we asserted that our motivation must be the love of God, the glory of God, and the love of disciples. At this juncture, it is appropriate to look again at the Great Commission and what is referred to by some as the 'New Commandment.'

> And Jesus came and said to them, "All authority in heaven and on earth has been given to me. Go therefore and make disciples of all nations, baptizing them in the name of the Father and of the Son and of the Holy Spirit, teaching them to observe all that I have commanded you. And behold, I am with you always, to the end of the age."[2]

---

[1] Cf. John 15:4-11 and Romans 12:1-2.
[2] Matthew 28:18-20.

He also commands "that you love one another: just as I have loved you, you also are to love one another. By this all people will know that you are my disciples, if you have love for one another."[3] In Chapter Seven we urged the development of a regimen of Christian Disciplines, the purpose of which is to deepen our love of God. This is in keeping with Jesus' Greatest Commandment to love God with all our heart, soul, mind and strength.[4] From this love and unity with God grows one's love for fellow disciples. In my own experience, that love for fellow disciples grows as a fruit of God working in me. I cannot conjure this love that Jesus describes, it must be the fruit of my personal discipleship with him. Consider Paul's word to the Philippians.

> For God is my witness, how I yearn for you all with the affection of Christ Jesus. And it is my prayer that your love may abound more and more, with knowledge and all discernment, so that you may approve what is excellent, and so be pure and blameless for the day of Christ, filled with the fruit of righteousness that comes through Jesus Christ, to the glory and praise of God.[5]

It is God's love flowing through me that causes any yearning to walk with other disciples. With this motivation, we turn to how that journey may take place. Let's consider a long-distance train ride. The train travels at high speed between stops. At each stop, passengers may disembark for a brief period of time to get a coffee, a takeaway meal, or just stretch their legs. During this pause on the longer trip one may find provision or refreshment. In this metaphor, our life is the railway journey and the stops are our disciple making conversations. The conversations are the provision, refreshment and exercising of one's gifts. With that, let's turn to the nature of the gathering and the conversation.

What is a Disciple Making Conversation and How Does It Start?

Practical examples in the last chapter demonstrate the means to work out one's own set of spiritual disciplines. To follow a personal discipleship

---

[3] John 13:34-35.
[4] Cf. Mark 12:29-31.
[5] Philippians 1:8-11.

regimen is to move forward in training of one's heart and mind. One's personal discipleship is, as we have stated already, not undertaken in isolation. The disciple needs to be engaged in community. Again, we quote Dallas Willard, who states. "Spiritual formation, good or bad, is always profoundly social. You cannot keep it to yourself."[6] Forsaking isolation, disciples gather for regular, vulnerable and honest conversation. This is centered around Scripture as a guide to following our Master, Jesus. These conversations are facilitated by meaningful questions among friends who are growing in Christ as they walk together. Optimally, these conversations are facilitated by the local congregation. When a congregation is serious about disciple making, it should help birth and nurture conversations.

The Local Congregation as the Incubator for Disciple Making

An incubator is a safe place where nourishment and growth are encouraged. The congregation is the natural place for disciple making to be nurtured. In the gathering of the people, friendships should be discovered and encouraged. In this section I will be referring to what is commonly called the local church using the word congregation.

Local congregations are essential to disciple making. They are gatherings of people who should, with a biblical understanding of Jesus' commands, want to be, and make, disciples. Developing disciples should be the natural fruit of a congregation's ministry. This is facilitated through teaching and preaching in the regular meetings and fostering the kind of friendships within the congregation advocated in this project. But, as we have asserted in previous chapters, disciples are not made from pulpits alone. Therefore, I have suggested the idea of the pulpit-table tandem. This idea creates a synergy between the weekly teaching and preaching of Scripture with the regular disciple making conversations of the people. This is nothing new. The Pietists, with their conventicles, were practitioners of the kind of biblically centered discussion about the life of following Christ. Thus, disciples of Jesus are made and sustained in community.

In the paradigm proposed here, a pastor's first priority is to teach and preach the Scriptures in such a way that God is glorified and the gospel is clear each week. Teachings are presented in such a way that they become a

---

[6] Dallas Willard, *Renovation of the Heart* (Colorado Springs, CO: NavPress, 2002), 182.

topic of every disciple making conversation. This can be done in many ways but I assert that the most meaningful method is when questions are created from the teaching that is readily available to disciples. These questions may best emerge in collaboration with people who have been identified as apt disciple makers. They will have a sense of how to ask questions that may be clearer than the preacher could pose. In the gathering of fellow disciples, these questions can be the centerpiece of the conversation, or can merely serve as a supplement. The speaker must be mindful of the need for such interaction as the sermon/teaching is prepared. The questions provided from the teaching should reflect biblical exegesis and clear application in the sermon. A congregation of disciples engaging in conversations guided by meaningful questions will move those people deeper into discipleship of Jesus. This will cause the preacher to think carefully about application of the sermon, perhaps a positive side effect of the process. These theological and applicative questions, during conversations, will help students of Jesus gain a deeper understanding of the teaching and help one another live out the teachings on a more personal level than is possible from a pulpit.

Fostering Friendships

Congregational leaders should actively facilitate the emergence of friendships that bloom into disciple making conversations within the body. Every culture and subculture will vary as to *how* leaders of congregations adapt this practice. Yet, I suggest that when leaders, from anywhere, set the example through engaging in disciple making conversations within their own circle and moving out from there, others may see the value more readily. As we grow in our personal discipleship, we can see the value of others investing in us. With this understanding, we then begin to engage with others in disciple making.

The local congregation should facilitate friendships that become disciple making conversations. To show how that may occur, I will borrow and adapt a practice of a congregation I have consulted with for some time. The pastoral staff gathers for a weekly meeting to discuss their observations from the most recent gathering of the congregation. In this meeting, they pool their observations to determine who may need of a phone call or visit. They consider who was absent, appears to be isolated, or gave the impression of being troubled. Their objective each week is to determine who needs to be approached for possible pastoral care.

If this team of pastors took that same pool of knowledge and considered those already gathering with fellow disciples, they may identify who is not engaging regularly in fellow disciple conversations. They can also use that information to consider how existing friendships may develop disciple making conversations. If the church has a leadership structure, i.e. elders or deacons, they should also be helpful resources to determine who is and is not connecting with others. In my observation, a program with slogans on banners lasts about as long as the banners. Set programs are not always the best method to develop long-term disciples. Rather, existing organic relationships among friends should breed disciple making conversations. Further, leaders should identify who is engaging in conversations already, thus determining who is in a gathering of disciples. How does this gathering naturally operate? What are the commonalities that have drawn together these fellow disciples? How many are there? Has a leader emerged? From this information, the congregational leadership guides this cluster of friends about disciple making. If there is room and if the leadership knows of a person who may fit the group naturally, that person can be proposed to the group.

Essentially, I am arguing that the pastor should become a disciple-maker in the pulpit and then around a table. He or she should invest some time each week to consider the people in the congregation and then set aside time each week to connect people into possible friendships that become disciple making in nature. Local adaptation is the key. There really is no cookie cutter to use. This is why the so-called McDonaldization of the church has been weighed and found lacking. A set program prepared by curriculum writers cannot consider the vast number and kind of variables to form the personality of a congregation. Rather, each congregation can quietly, organically and slowly begin moving its focus into spiritual development among friends. These friends make other friends and they too engage in disciple making conversations. Over time, many or most of the congregants should emerge as disciple-makers. As God guides and blesses, multiplication may take place in the congregation. But it will be broadening through depth not shallowness. Congregations may then become a mile wide because they are a mile deep.

The Nature of and the Number in Disciple Making Conversations

Like the personal discipleship description in Chapter Seven, this section will be a synthesis of my own experience and what has emerged from our research thus far. Each practitioner must adapt these ideas into his or her own cultural context as one develops a disciple making regimen. Let's consider the optimal number of persons in these conversations.

There can be too few in a conversation. A regular meeting of two is likely to develop into a mentor-protégé relationship. This occurs because of differences in experience age and the type of education each one has. This would be helpful for both, but it is not quite as duplicatable since the protégé does not have as much opportunity to develop with those less experienced. There can also be too many in attendance. Lewis warned us against a caucus.[7] In my experience, the best gatherings for fellow disciple conversations are from three to five in number. More than five is more difficult to host and limits how much each one may participate.

Let me also make clear that I am not advocating what are widely known as 'cells,' 'fellowship groups' or 'small groups.' They are frequently used as a means toward a church-growth paradigm. Groups of this kind serve their purpose but are often too large, are mixed gender and operate like small congregations. These factors do not facilitate the kind of conversations advocated in this project. 'Small group' ministry has its place, especially in caring for families, but it is not what is advocated here.

Where?

Where the group meets is important. My own experience of successful and fruitful conversations flavors my conclusions and therefore the reader who puts these suggestions into practice must contextualize to his or her own sub-culture. I have found that the location should have consistency. The same cafe for breakfast, the same porch for coffee, or the same backyard for lunch or tea can all serve just as well. It could be as simple a cup of coffee on a park bench, but regularity of time and location provides a helpful degree of familiarity. Having the meeting at the same agreed upon time and place each week gives the participants something to plan on and look forward to. Familiarity of place enables the attention of the disciples to be on the conversation rather than being distracted by a constantly changing landscape.

---

[7] C. S. Lewis, "Membership" in *The Weight of Glory* (New York: MacMillan, 1949; repr., Grand Rapids, MI: William B. Eerdmans, 1979), 30-31.

Using Questions in Disciple Making

From our study of Jesus' method in Chapter 7 we learned the value of astute questions. Os Guinness deftly states that "questions are involving. Whereas a statement always has a "take it or leave it" quality, and we may or may not be interested in what it tells us, there is no standing back from a well-asked question."[8] Questions and answers are essential in this proposal. Asking questions is more art than science. Over the years, God has helped me learn how to ask questions. Through many experiences and influences it became clear to me that the best way to learn about someone was to ask questions about his or her story. I have observed that a helpful question has several characteristics.

First, it is based on the conversation thus far and on the other person's participation. This requires listening. Developing these skills is a vital early step. Next, the incisive question is close enough to the stream of conversation that it adds to or guides the discussion without derailing it. It may supplement a point or it may be used to shift the subject slightly. A thoughtful question may include an element of surprise. This is helpful in provoking thought.

One must, as we observe in Jesus, pay close attention. Giving due notice in a discussion today means preventing our phones from interrupting. To give another person one's undivided attention in a face to face, honest conversation is an incredible gift, turning off our phone makes this possible. This is especially true in today's social media driven world where we look into computer and smartphone screens far more than we sit face to face with another person. A further characteristic of a good question is a thoughtful pause after the question has been asked. The person to whom the question is addressed often needs time to think. I had to learn to be patient so that my friend could ponder the question. Questions should make us think. We need to give one another time to think. A helpful question needs background. To have a growing knowledge of one another's biography is a sign of a growing friendship. We discover friendship where we find common interest. It is developed in face to face conversations. This growing friendship is love for fellow disciples.

---

[8] Os Guinness, *Fool's Talk* (Downers Grove, IL: InterVarsity, 2015), 52.

Applicative Questions

What are three examples from your life where someone has asked you a question that caused you to reexamine your thinking on a matter?

List three people whom you consider friends, with whom you have social relationships, and common interests.

Invite one of these friends for lunch and ask them some careful questions about faith. Look for the opportunity to invite this person to join you in an exploration of Jesus. You might use the "Essential Jesus" reading plan from YouVersion as the scriptural basis for this conversation.

CHAPTER SIXTEEN

QUESTIONS IN CONVERSATION

Disciple Making Friendships

Augustine, Aquinas and Lewis demonstrated the importance of friendships through books letters and around tables. One of the ongoing conversations that strengthens me meets every week on a porch. Sometimes one of our group is absent and our host will invite another person to join the conversation. His hope is that others will catch the desire for fellow disciple making. On these occasions, my own participation in the conversation becomes muted. An introvert by nature, I always thought it was because I am shy. I see, however, that it is something else altogether. In order to really participate in a significant conversation, I need to listen and understand the context of their lives before I enter in. Gaining understanding about one another is a gradual process that happens over time. This leads to another aspect of good questions. They are asked in the context ongoing regular, vulnerable and honest conversations. To these facets of a disciple making conversation we now turn.

Vulnerable and Honest

When I urge vulnerability in conversations, I am saying that we need a willingness to open ourselves to fellow disciples by sharing our own struggles, perhaps even to the point of revealing what may shock some. It is only through openly sharing our sin and asking for help that we can point one another to the love of the Father for us, the work of Christ on the cross, and the guidance of the Holy Spirit in us. In this context, Willard confirms the importance of confession, stating that it operates "within fellowship." He goes on to say that "in it we let trusted others know our deepest weaknesses and failures."[1] This will not happen without vulnerability. There is no

---

[1] Dallas Willard, *Spirit of the Disciplines* (New York: HarperCollins, 1988), 187.

confession apart from vulnerability. Honest conversations are integral to vulnerable conversations. When people in a vulnerable conversation are open to sharing, an honest conversation is truthful and prone to fruitfulness. In the last chapter I suggested that a tool to aid in this for leaders (and all disciples for that matter) can be found in Appendix E. It is not an end all but could provide the kind of beginning for conversations that we sometimes need. It is easier for my friend to see and point out my pride than for me to see it myself. We might remain closed until we feel safe, but when we speak, we should be truthful. Invulnerability is like a wall around each person's heart and mind. Their life experience has built this wall and for some it is high, for others it is lower, for some it is high and quite thick. In my experience, climbing over this wall requires a commitment to the person through regular conversations. It also takes patience. One cannot force vulnerability any more than one can push a rope.

While being honest and vulnerable is the goal, in newer friendships, vulnerability must be given time to grow. This process takes trust and trust, as they say, is earned. The organization in which I serve has used a specific introductory disciple making course[2] with remarkable success. It is a nine-session conversation that is based on Scripture, an essay, and thoughtful questions. I have been privileged to go through it with over 50 ministry partners. When establishing relationships with people new to our ministry, I work hard to get a sense of how vulnerable they are willing to be. My practice is to dive as deep as they are willing. There have been persons who took several weeks to get to what I deemed a healthy willingness to share their hearts. Others are more naturally open. One brother had no hesitation to dive deep into vulnerable territory. We could get into deeply meaningful conversations immediately because he was willing to trust and be vulnerable. We must pray for discernment to know how fast we may proceed and for the patience to wait as did our Lord Jesus. To that end, vulnerable and honest conversations require time and constancy.

Regular

Under normal circumstances, the openness we seek will come from regular discussions. Establishing a dependable frequency of conversation

---

[2] Bob Thune and Will Walker, *Gospel Centered Life* (Philadelphia: World Harvest Mission, 2009), iv.

deepens the knowledge that friends have about one another. Regularity builds a bond that enhances trust. The very best conversations between fellow disciples happen over a longer period of time and with a frequency of no fewer than two conversations than twice monthly. Generally, to meet less frequently suppresses the kind of consistency needed for openness that is vital in these conversations. This is because after an absence, too much time is spent getting caught up on recent life events. This leaves less time getting to the heart of matters to which Scripture can speak. We are describing a commitment, and even a submission, to enter a relationship whose goal is to point one another to the gospel. Fellow disciples meet to engage in conversation that, as Willard describes, involves "humility, complete honesty, transparency, and at times confession and restitution."[3] In focusing on this, I am emphasizing the need for regular meeting. There are walls that keep us apart. Walls of insecurity, of hurt and of sin. It is through regular time together that we slowly climb over those walls into the realm of vulnerability. It is in a spirit of submission that I join my friends regularly to listen attentively and speak openly. It is through vulnerability and honesty that I can confess my sins as my fellow disciples remind me of the gospel. Indeed, for leaders, regular consideration of balance in life is imperative. In Appendix E one may see a device to aid in this examination of one's own life and submitting that examination to fellow disciples. Through this examination, our fellow disciples may shine the light of the gospel into our hearts. It is that gospel centeredness that points us to our next facet, these conversations must be centered in the Scriptures.

Bible Centered

Earlier, we stated that one role of the leader of the disciple making congregation is to teach and preach in such a way that there could be discussion of that teaching among fellow disciples. This is what we are calling the pulpit-table tandem. It is at the heart of a congregation based disciple making paradigm. Indeed, every disciple making conversation should have Scripture at its center. The Word of God should be at the heart of the conversation. This means that in every conversation, we should read and apply the text to the matter at hand. Biblical theology preached from the pulpit, studied in our homes, and discussed among fellow disciples is essential

---

[3] Willard, *Spirit of the Disciplines*, 189.

to deepening our understanding of, and relationship with God. Consider the assertion of the Prince of Preachers from 19th Century London, C. H. Spurgeon. He stated that "those who do away with Christian doctrine are, whether they are aware of it or not, the worst enemies of Christian living ... [because] the coals of orthodoxy are necessary to the fire of piety."[4] No clearer words may be spoken to remind us of the vital importance of making Scripture the heart of our conversations.

This does not, however, imply that we should engage in an Inductive Bible Study. These types of Bible studies are extremely helpful in their place but are didactic in nature and may be most profitable as a parallel to our disciple making conversations. Our goal is to use questions that probe hearts and elicit responses. Scripture speaks into those responses. This requires there to be at least one member of the group familiar enough with Scripture to be able to speak to issues raised, or be mature enough to be able to delay that aspect of the conversation until proper biblical answers may be acquired. This also suggests that there should not be three brand new disciples trying to lead one another. In this case of not-yet-mature disciples, the seven questions paradigm used in Disciple Making Movements[5] may be recommended.[6] But they will need oversight, perhaps as a more mature disciple is available for consultation. What about the ages in a group?

Mixing Generations

The questions of mixing generations and mixing experience are not easy to answer. Generally, I find that mixing generations *can* work depending on the group and the ability of the fellow disciples to honor one another. To expect the cultural context of a thirty-something to be understood by someone in his or her sixties or seventies, however, may be unreasonable. In my observation, as cultures change, it is often older people who resist the change and the younger participants who embrace it. This can make for lively

---

[4] Erroll Hulse and David Kingdon, eds., *A Marvelous Ministry: How the All-round Ministry of Charles Haddon Spurgeon Speaks to Us Today* (Grand Rapids, MI: Soli Deo Gloria Publications, 1993), 128.

[5] See a form of the Disciple Making Movement questions in Appendix B.

[6] Timothy Keller, *Preaching* (New York: Viking, 2015) is a valuable resource for one who is leading a group of not yet experienced disciples.

and enlightening discussion, but does it facilitate the kind of openness and vulnerability that we rely on? This does not mean that a sixty-year-old leader cannot engage a twenty-something in a one-on-one friendship for disciple making. But, again, that scenario may become more of a mentoring relationship. This mentor-protégé model is helpful as the mentor might work with the protégé especially in the earlier situation where three equally inexperienced disciples are meeting together.

Mixing Genders?

Regular disciple making conversations should be single gender. There are, of course, valid exceptions to this. In my role as a facilitator of teachers and a kind of pastor to pastors, I do have disciple making conversations with women. But this is not the fellow disciple making being advocated here because it includes professional mentoring. Indeed, a pastoral ministry does necessitate inter-gender conversations. I often meet with married couples associated with my ministry. But those discussions are hybrids of fellow disciple making, mentoring and often including pastoral counselling. In what this project proposes, mixing genders is not recommended. In my own experience, this allows more freedom and vulnerability for honest discussions about various issues of life, especially with respect to sexual sin. Doesn't prudence suggest that those conversations take place between persons of the same gender?

Disciple Making as Outreach

When we examine Jesus' method, we observe that there are many who are referred to as disciples who had not believed. This raises the question about disciple making among those yet-to-believe. This subject was touched upon in the previous chapter with my own experience of being 'discipled into belief. Disciple making as outreach is the basis of the Disciple Making Movements mentioned previously. The objective it to engage with people in regular Bible reading, prayer and conversation about the biblical text, using questions and answers to guide conversation around the Scripture. This brings people into an understanding of and response to the gospel. In this way, these persons are, similar to my own experience, discipled into belief. They turn to Christ as Savior as they meet regularly with others. Of those with whom they meet, at least one is a believer and may be the facilitator of the gathering. But he or she is not teaching the text as much as asking the seven questions[7] and participating in the conversation based on the text and its application. Missiologist Ted Esler provides instructive perspective on the movement as a paradigm of evangelism and contrasts it with proclamation based models.[8] In our inquiry about discipling people into belief, suffice it to say that in cultures that are steeped in postmodern thought and, to an increasing degree, culturally post-Christian, this friendship based model may have great appeal for those wishing to use disciple making as outreach. But it is not, in my assessment, the clearest way forward for long-term fellow disciple making. For the purposes of this project, that system is somewhat formulaic and can become static. It is, however, an incredibly valuable tool for community outreach. What are some ways that disciple making may be used as outreach?

Community Outreach

As we consider ways in which disciple making can influence those around us we should look to our existing friendships asking: From which of my friendships can I see disciple making emerge? With that in mind, we may invite these friends to join us in a regular gathering to look at life and Scripture together. In these conversations, we point one another to Jesus. The next circle out is our professional colleagues and civic organizations. We may gather with these friends at lunch or after work to discuss the way that our work affects our lives and how the gospel informs that living. The next layer of relationships may be our neighbors who, in our modern culture, we may not know very well. Visiting with them to discover commonalities over a meal can lead to a new friendship. That new relationship may become a disciple making conversation in your neighborhood. While not specifically about disciple making as in our proposal, Alan Briggs, a pastor and church planting facilitator, has written a particularly helpful book in this area: *Staying is the New*

---

[7] Cf. Appendix B: "The Seven Question Method."

[8] Ted Esler, "Two Church Planting Paradigms" in *International Journal of Frontier Missiology*, 30:2 Summer 2013, 67-73, www.ijfm.org/PDFs_IJFM/30_2_PDFs/IJFM_30_2-Esler.pdf (accessed 7-19-16).

Going.[9]

In a large economics university in a central European capital, a lecturer in the social sciences regularly takes students into settings where they serve others. They work in homes for the handicapped and orphanages. In educational parlance, this is called Service Learning. But his goal is the establishment of meaningful conversations with these students. This model could easily develop into disciple making conversations. The same is true for organizations whose mission is social justice. Essentially, for Kingdom advancement, disciple making as outreach is a means to bring people together and reach out to those in their circles that have yet to meet Christ.

Fulfilling the Great Commission

Once those relationships are established and these new disciples begin to learn about Jesus, they may then be introduced to the wider community of believers in the congregation. In this way, naturally, the gospel is going forth. As disciples are strengthened, the church grows deeper, not just wider. As we go along our regular way, we should help others to become students of Jesus. We fulfill the Great Commission by making disciples.

---

[9] Alan Briggs, *Staying is the New Going* (Colorado Springs: NavPress, 2015).

Applicative Questions

Ask your pastor to introduce you to someone in your local congregation who seems isolated. Invite them to lunch and ask about their life to get to know them. As you get to know them, you will be able to ask questions about a Scripture that you recently found meaningful. Ask them for their perspective on how to apply the sermon from the latest gathering.

Ask your church leadership to connect you to two or three others who are not yet gathering in disciple making conversation. Begin meeting every two weeks in a regular place at a mutually agreeable time.

CONCLUSION

In the Introduction, we read of a congregation in Eastern Europe. As a kind of closing exercise, let's rethink that story. The pastor and his wife, who we'll call Eva, each identify two persons from the church that they believe would be interested in meeting regularly for coffee and discussion. The pastor asks his wife to help him develop questions from the Sunday teaching of God's word. These questions and coffee are on the table each week as they begin to invest regularly in these two pairs of leaders. As each group gets to know one another, the groups slowly climb from invulnerability to real honesty.

As these groups continue to meet, each person is urged to pray about who they could invite to join the group. The wife's group grows from the initial three to four and then five. One of the original two women has demonstrated real growth in discernment and has been given the opportunity to lead the group step by step. As other women learn about what is happening, Eva leaves the leadership of the first group and begins another group, taking with her the other original group member with her. In this new group, the woman who had been in the original group is given leadership opportunities immediately. She takes the questions from the sermon each week and faithfully guides the conversation. When the mission team arrives the following summer, there are women that have grown deeper in their knowledge of Scripture and are walking more closely with the Lord. They take a more active role in the work with the families attracted by the mission team's efforts. Rather than being exhausted by the ministry with the mission team, they are invigorated and two new women, mothers of vising children, begin meeting in the disciple making groups. Their influence on their families fosters the children's regular attendance in Bible club.

The men are another story. After several attempts to meet with men in the church, the Pastor, who we will call Peter, finds that the men on the church are not as interested as the women. Peter consults with another pastor who suggests he look outside the church instead and begin using the seven-question method (Appendix B). He begins meeting separately with two men and reading through the Praying Scripture list (Appendix D) and using the seven questions of coffee. After a few months of conversations and a fishing trip where the three men get to know one another, they finally begin to climb over the wall of invulnerability into honesty. Peter continues to seek to involve men in the church but is content that these two men are getting to know Jesus. On Easter, both men come to church with their families and become part of the community. When the mission team arrives, they discover that there are almost a dozen men and women who are meeting as fellow disciples. The efforts of the mission team in their English camp are doubled as the visitors to this program find a warm welcome from these disciples of Jesus.

At the final dinner, there is not a sermon, but two testimonies, one from a man and one from a woman of how God is working in their lives through a caring community of believers. Afterward, there are three conversations with guests who are interested in knowing how to become part of a such a group.

This story is still fictitious. The elements of our little story, however, are based in reality. Stories like the one in the Introduction and its updated version here, emerged from real life and provide the vision for this project. This research examined the lack of robust faith, explored plausible causes both historically and theologically and finally put forth a solution. The purpose behind the objective was twofold. First, the research would increase my own expertise on the subject so that I could continue to urge disciple making through my work domestically and abroad. Secondly, it would produce a text that I can use in my work to try to instill this knowledge, and hopefully vision, in the leaders with whom I connect on a regular basis as well as a manual to use in training new ministry partners. Throughout, I have prayed two prayers, First, that God would guide the work and second that He would use it to advance His Kingdom.

I was surprised by the way this research took on a direction of its own. I did not expect to find so much helpful information about disciple making throughout Christian history. In the writings of Antony, Augustine, Aquinas, Luther, Spener, Lewis and others, a vast wealth exists urging us on to a deeper union with God and a biblical understanding of God. In the writings of great theologians, of Mystics, and of others with mystical leanings we see the vital nature of biblical theology and union with God through devotion. Spurgeon expresses it well saying that "the coals of orthodoxy are necessary to the fire of piety"[10] This is the answer to the question posed at the beginning. What is discipleship? The marriage of biblical theology and unity with God.

Through this research, we have sought answers to the questions proposed at the outset. Why did discipleship exist so sacrificially, and then fade? Why is it largely missing today and what can be done to correct the problem? We have sought to clarify the difference between 'discipleship' and 'disciple making.' 'Discipleship' may now be less ambiguous, though it will remain ubiquitous for the foreseeable future. We have suggested the importance of 'disciple making' in advancing God's Kingdom. From this research, a clearer understanding of the Matthean Great Commission has been gained. An unambiguous picture emerged of what Jesus meant when He told us to make disciples. Perhaps most surprising and helpful to the development of my practice of disciple making is the discovery of the historical and pedagogical context of Jesus. What emerged from the study of His question and answer method in the Synoptics was another aspect of contextualization. Of particular interest was the Greek and Rabbinic contextual influences that He worked with as He made disciples.

In the end, the objective is achieved. A biblical, duplicatable, and (largely) culturally adaptable model for 'disciple making' has been recommended. It is, according to our goal, flexible for most cultural contexts. It is simple. It is biblical. It does not need a conference nor a training series on DVD to learn because it is learned naturally within one's existing congregation and circle of friends.

With this research, I see what will be the focus of my remaining ministry years: disciple making and the fostering of disciple makers. In this, as God guides, local congregations will have a tool to avoid what Stott calls "growth without depth."[11] With this fresher understanding, our journey continues with fellow disciples in conversations that lead us to make disciples who glorify God.

---

[10] Erroll Hulse and David Kingdon, eds., *A Marvelous Ministry: How the All-round Ministry of Charles Haddon Spurgeon Speaks to Us Today* (Grand Rapids, MI: Soli Deo Gloria Publications, 1993), 128.

[11] John Stott, *The Radical Disciple: Some Neglected Aspects of Our Calling* (Downers Grove, IL: InterVarsityPress, 2012), kindle, location 278.

APPENDICES

THE QUESTIONS OF JESUS FROM THE SYNOPTICS

ref #	Matthew (87) Mark (78) Luke (112) Reference numbers (ref #) mark a separate event or change of topic in a sermon, not necessarily the order of sequence.
1	"You are the salt of the earth, but if salt has lost its taste, how shall its saltiness be restored? It is no longer good for anything except to be thrown out and trampled under people's feet." Matthew 5:13
2	"For if you love those who love you, what reward do you have? Do not even the tax collectors do the same? And if you greet only your brothers, what more are you doing than others? Do not even the Gentiles do the same?" Matthew 5:46-47
3	"But if God so clothes the grass of the field, which today is alive and tomorrow is thrown into the oven, will he not much more clothe you, O you of little faith?" Matthew 6:30
4	"But Jesus, knowing their thoughts, said, "Why do you think evil in your hearts?" For which is easier, to say, 'Your sins are forgiven,' or to say, 'Rise and walk'? Matthew 9:4-5

"And immediately Jesus, perceiving in his spirit that they thus questioned within themselves, said to them, 'Why do you question these things in your hearts? Which is easier, to say to the paralytic, 'Your sins are forgiven,' or to say, 'Rise, take up your bed and walk'?" Mark 2:8-9

"When Jesus perceived their thoughts, he answered them, "Why do you question in your hearts? Which is easier, to say, 'Your sins are forgiven you,' or to say, 'Rise and walk'?" Luke 5:22-23 |

| 5 | "And Jesus said to them, "Can the wedding guests fast while the bridegroom is with them? As long as they have the bridegroom with them, they cannot fast." Mark 2:19

"And Jesus said to them, "Can you make wedding guests fast while the bridegroom is with them?" Luke 5:34 |
|---|---|
| 6 | "He said to them, "Have you not read what David did when he was hungry, and those who were with him: how he entered the house of God and ate the bread of the Presence, which it was not lawful for him to eat nor for those who were with him, but only for the priests? Or have you not read in the Law how on the Sabbath the priests in the temple profane the Sabbath and are guiltless? Matthew 12:3-5

"And he said to them, "Have you never read what David did, when he was in need and was hungry, he and those who were with him: how he entered the house of God, in the time of Abiathar the high priest, and ate the bread of the Presence, which it is not lawful for any but the priests to eat, and also gave it to those who were with him?" Mark 2:25-26

"And Jesus answered them, "Have you not read what David did when he was hungry, he and those who were with him: how he entered the house of God and took and ate the bread of the Presence, which is not lawful for any but the priests to eat, and also gave it to those with him?" Luke 6:3-4 |
| 7 | "Is it lawful on the Sabbath to do good or to do harm, to save life or to kill?" But they were silent." Mark 3:4

"And Jesus said to them, "I ask you, is it lawful on the Sabbath to do good or to do harm, to save life or to destroy it?" Luke 6:9 |
| 8 | "And he called them to him and said to them in parables, "How can Satan cast out Satan? ... And he answered them, "Who are my mother and my brothers?" Mark 3:23, 33

"And if Satan also is divided against himself, how will his kingdom stand? For you say that I cast out demons by Beelzebul. And if I cast out demons by Beelzebul, by whom do your sons cast them out?." Luke 11:18-19 |

9	"Why do you see the speck that is in your brother's eye, but do not notice the log that is in your own eye? Or how can you say to your brother, 'Let me take the speck out of your eye,' when there is the log in your own eye?" Matthew 7:3-4
	"Why do you see the speck that is in your brother's eye, but do not notice the log that is in your own eye? How can you say to your brother, 'Brother, let me take out the speck that is in your eye,' when you yourself do not see the log that is in your own eye? You hypocrite, first take the log out of your own eye, and then you will see clearly to take out the speck that is in your brother's eye." Luke 6:41-42
10	"Or which one of you, if his son asks him for bread, will give him a stone? Or if he asks for a fish, will give him a serpent?" Matthew 7:9-10
11	"And he said to them, "Do you not understand this parable? How then will you understand all the parables?" Mark 4:13
12	"You will recognize them by their fruits. Are grapes gathered from thornbushes, or figs from thistles?" Matthew 7:16
13	""Why do you call me 'Lord, Lord,' and not do what I tell you?" Luke 6:46
14	"And he said to them, "Is a lamp brought in to be put under a basket, or under a bed, and not on a stand?" Mark 4:21
15	And he said, "With what can we compare the kingdom of God, or what parable shall we use for it?" Mark 4:30
	"He said therefore, "What is the kingdom of God like? And to what shall I compare it? ... And again he said, "To what shall I compare the kingdom of God?" Luke 13:18, 20

16	"And he said to them, "Why are you afraid, O you of little faith?" Matthew 8:26 "And he said to them, "Why are still so afraid? Have you still no faith?" Mark 4:40 "He said to them, "Where is your faith?" Luke 8:25
17	"And Jesus asked him, "What is your name?" Mark 5:9 ESV "Jesus then asked him, "What is your name?" Luke 8:30 ESV
18	"When John's messengers had gone, Jesus began to speak to the crowds concerning John: "What did you go out into the wilderness to see? A reed shaken by the wind? What then did you go out to see? A man dressed in soft clothing? Behold, those who are dressed in splendid clothing and live in luxury are in kings' courts. What then did you go out to see? A prophet?" Luke 7:24-26
19	"But to what shall I compare this generation?" Matthew 11:16 "To what then shall I compare the people of this generation, and what are they like?" Luke 7:31
20	"And you, Capernaum, will you be exalted to heaven?" Matthew 11:23 "And you, Capernaum, will you be exalted to heaven?" Luke 10:15
21	"Do you believe that I am able to do this?" Matthew 9:28
22	"Are not two sparrows sold for a penny?" Matthew 10:29
23	"Now which of them will love him more?" … "Do you see this woman?" Luke 7:42, 44
24	"Who touched my garments?" Mark 5:31 "And Jesus said, "Who was it that touched me?" Luke 8:45

25	"Why are you making a commotion and weeping? The child is not dead but sleeping."" Mark 5:39
26	"Have you understood all these things?" Matthew 13:51
27	"O you of little faith, why did you doubt?" Matthew 14:31
28	"And why do you break the commandment of God for the sake of your tradition?" Matthew 15:3
29	"Are you also still without understanding? Do you not see that whatever goes into the mouth passes into the stomach and is expelled?" Matthew 15:16-17 "And he said to them, "Then are you also without understanding? Do you not see that whatever goes into a person from outside cannot defile him, since it enters not his heart but his stomach, and is expelled?" (Thus he declared all foods clean.)" Mark 7:18-19
30	"How many loaves do you have?" Matthew 15:34 "How many loaves do you have?" Mark 8:5
31	"Why does this generation seek a sign?" Mark 8:12
32	"O you of little faith, why are you discussing among yourselves the fact that you have no bread? Do you not yet perceive? Do you not remember the five loaves for the five thousand, and how many baskets you gathered? Or the seven loaves for the four thousand, and how many baskets you gathered? How is it that you fail to understand that I did not speak about bread?" Matthew 16:8-11 "Why are you discussing the fact that you have no bread? Do you not yet perceive or understand? Are your hearts hardened? Having eyes do you not see, and having ears do you not hear? And do you not remember? When I broke the five loaves for the five thousand, how many baskets full of broken pieces did you take up?" They said to him, "Twelve." "And the seven for the four thousand, how many baskets full of broken pieces did you take up?" … "Do you not yet understand?"" Mark 8:17-21

33	"Do you see anything?" Mark 8:23
34	"Who do people say that the Son of Man is?" … "But who do you say that I am?" Matthew 16:13, 15 "Who do people say that I am?"… "But who do you say that I am?" Mark 8:27, 29 "Who do the crowds say that I am?" … "But who do you say that I am?" Luke 9:18, 20
35	"For what will it profit a man if he gains the whole world and forfeits his soul? … Or what shall a man give in return for his soul?" Matt. 16:26
36	"And Jesus answered, "O faithless and twisted generation, how long am I to be with you? How long am I to bear with you?" Matthew 17:17 "What are you arguing about with them?" … "O faithless generation, 'how long am I to be with you? How long am I to bear with you?'" Mark 9:16, 19 "O faithless and twisted generation, how long am I to be with you and bear with you?" Luke 9:41
37	"What do you think, Simon? From whom do kings of the earth take toll or tax? From their sons or from others?" Matthew 17:25
38	"What were you discussing on the way?" … "If anyone would be first, he must be last of all and servant of all." Mark 9:33, 35
39	"What do you think? If a man has a hundred sheep, and one of them has gone astray, does he not leave the ninety-nine on the mountains and go in search of the one that went astray?" Matthew 18:12
40	"He said to him, "What is written in the Law? How do you read it?" Luke 10:26

41	"Are not five sparrows sold for two pennies? And not one of them is forgotten before God. Why, even the hairs of your head are all numbered. Fear not; you are of more value than many sparrows." Luke 12:6-7
42	"But he said to him, "Man, who made me a judge or arbitrator over you?" ... "What shall I do, for I have nowhere to store my crops?" ... But God said to him, 'Fool! This night your soul is required of you, and the things you have prepared, whose will they be?'" ... "And which of you by being anxious can add a single hour to his span of life? If then you are not able to do as small a thing as that, why are you anxious about the rest?" Luke 12:14, 17, 20-21, 25-26 "Who then is the faithful and wise manager, whom his master will set over his household, to give them their portion of food at the proper time?" Luke 12:42 "Do you think that I have come to give peace on earth? No, I tell you, but rather division." Luke 12:51
43	"Do you think that these Galileans were worse sinners than all the other Galileans, because they suffered in this way?... Or those eighteen on whom the tower in Siloam fell and killed them: do you think that they were worse offenders than all the others who lived in Jerusalem?" Luke 13:2, 4
44	"Does not each of you on the Sabbath untie his ox or his donkey from the manger and lead it away to water it? And ought not this woman, a daughter of Abraham whom Satan bound for eighteen years, be loosed from this bond on the Sabbath day?" Luke 13:15-16
45	"Is it lawful to heal on the Sabbath, or not?" ... "Which of you, having a son or an ox that has fallen into a well on a Sabbath day, will not immediately pull him out?"" Luke 14:3, 5
46	"For which of you, desiring to build a tower, does not first sit down and count the cost, whether he has enough to complete it? Otherwise, when he has laid a foundation and is not able to finish, all who see it begin to mock him, saying, 'This man began to build and was not able to finish.' Or what king, going out to encounter another king in war, will not sit down first and deliberate whether he is able with ten thousand to meet him who comes against him with twenty thousand?" Luke 14:28-31

47	"What man of you, having a hundred sheep, if he has lost one of them, does not leave the ninety-nine in the open country, and go after the one that is lost, until he finds it?...Or what woman, having ten silver coins, if she loses one coin, does not light a lamp and sweep the house and seek diligently until she finds it?" Luke 15:4, 8
48	"Will any one of you who has a servant plowing or keeping sheep say to him when he has come in from the field, 'Come at once and recline at table'? Will he not rather say to him, 'Prepare supper for me, and dress properly, and serve me while I eat and drink, and afterward you will eat and drink'? Does he thank the servant because he did what was commanded?" Luke 17:7-9
49	"Were not ten cleansed? Where are the nine? Was no one found to return and give praise to God except this foreigner?" Luke 17:17-19
50	"And will not God give justice to his elect, who cry to him day and night? Will he delay long over them? I tell you, he will give justice to them speedily. Nevertheless, when the Son of Man comes, will he find faith on earth?" Luke 18:6-8
51	"What did Moses command you?" Mark 10:3
52	"And should not you have had mercy on your fellow servant, as I had mercy on you?' Matthew 18:33
53	"Have you not read that he who created them from the beginning made them male and female, and said, 'Therefore a man shall leave his father and his mother and hold fast to his wife, and the two shall become one flesh'?" Matthew 19:4-5
54	"Why do you ask me about what is good?" Matthew 19:17

"Why do you call me good?" Mark 10:18

"Why do you call me good?" Luke 18:19 |

55	"Why do you stand here idle all day?" … "Did you not agree with me for a denarius?" … "Am I not allowed to do what I choose with what belongs to me?" … "Or do you begrudge my generosity?" Matthew 20:6, 13, 15
56	"What do you want?" … "Are you able to drink the cup that I am to drink?" Matthew 20:21-22 "What do you want me to do for you?" … "Are you able to drink the cup that I drink, or to be baptized with the baptism with which I am baptized?" Mark 10:36, 38 "For who is the greater, one who reclines at table or one who serves? Is it not the one who reclines at table?" Luke 22:27
57	"was the baptism of John from heaven or from man?" Luke 20:4
58	"What do you want me to do for you?" Matthew 20:32 "What do you want me to do for you?" Mark 10:51 "What do you want me to do for you?" Luke 18:41
59	"Yes; have you never read, 'Out of the mouth of infants and nursing babies you have prepared praise'?" Matthew 21:16
60	"What do you think? A man had two sons. And he went to the first and said, 'Son, go and work in the vineyard today.' And he answered, 'I will not,' but afterward he changed his mind and went. And he went to the other son and said the same. And he answered, 'I go, sir,' but did not go. Which of the two did the will of his father?" Matthew 21:28-31

| 61 | "When therefore the owner of the vineyard comes, what will he do to those tenants?" ... "Have you never read in the Scriptures: 'The stone that the builders rejected has become the cornerstone; this was the Lord's doing, and it is marvelous in our eyes'?" Matthew 21:40-42

"Have you not read this Scripture: '"The stone that the builders rejected has become the cornerstone; this was the Lord's doing, and it is marvelous in our eyes'?"" Mark 12:10-11

"What then is this that is written: 'The stone that the builders rejected has become the cornerstone'? Everyone who falls on that stone will be broken to pieces, and when it falls on anyone, it will crush him." Luke 20:17-18 |
|---|---|
| 62 | "Whose likeness and inscription does it have?" Luke 20:24 |
| 63 | "And he said to him, 'Friend, how did you get in here without a wedding garment?" Matthew 22:12 |
| 64 | "Is this not the reason you are wrong, because you know neither the Scriptures nor the power of God? For when they rise from the dead, they neither marry nor are given in marriage, but are like angels in heaven. And as for the dead being raised, have you not read in the book of Moses, in the passage about the bush, how God spoke to him, saying, 'I am the God of Abraham, and the God of Isaac, and the God of Jacob'?" Mark 12:24-27 |
| 65 | "How can they say that the Christ is David's son? For David himself says in the Book of Psalms, '"The Lord said to my Lord, "Sit at my right hand, until I make your enemies your footstool."' David thus calls him Lord, so how is he his son?'" Luke 20:41-44 |
| 66 | "You see all these, do you not?" Matthew 24:2

"Do you see these great buildings?" Mark 13:2 |
| 67 | "Why do you trouble her?" Mark 14:6 |
| 68 | "When I sent you out with no moneybag or knapsack or sandals, did you lack anything?" ... Luke 22:35 |

69	"So, could you not watch with me one hour?" Matthew 26:40
	"Simon, are you asleep? Could you not watch one hour?" Mark 14:37
	"Why are you sleeping?" Luke 22:46
70	Do you think that I cannot appeal to my Father, and he will at once send me more than twelve legions of angels? But how then should the Scriptures be fulfilled, that it must be so?" … "Have you come out as against a robber, with swords and clubs to capture me?" Matthew 26: 53. 54, 55
	"Have you come out as against a robber, with swords and clubs to capture me?" Mark 14:48
	"Have you come out as against a robber, with swords and clubs?" Luke 22:52
71	"For behold, the days are coming when they will say, 'Blessed are the barren and the wombs that never bore and the breasts that never nursed!' Then they will begin to say to the mountains, 'Fall on us,' and to the hills, 'Cover us.' For if they do these things when the wood is green, what will happen when it is dry?" Luke 23:29-31

	From the cross forward, He kept asking questions:
	"And about the ninth hour Jesus cried out with a loud voice, saying, 'Eli, Eli, lema sabachthani?' that is, 'My God, my God, why have you forsaken me?'" Matthew 27:46

"And at the ninth hour Jesus cried with a loud voice, 'Eloi, Eloi, lema sabachthani?' which means, 'My God, my God, why have you forsaken me?'" Mark 15:34 |
| | "What is this conversation that you are holding with each other as you walk?" ... "What things?" Luke 24:17, 19

"Was it not necessary that the Christ should suffer these things and enter into his glory?" Luke 24:26

"Why are you troubled, and why do doubts arise in your hearts?" Luke 24:38

"Have you anything here to eat?" Luke 24:41

"Saul, Saul, why are you persecuting me?" Acts 9:4 |

APPENDIX B

SPIRITUAL DISCIPLINES

Foster	Willard	Keller
meditation	solitude	Bible study
prayer	silence	Bible reading
fasting	fasting	Bible meditation
study	frugality	adoration prayer
simplicity	chastity	confession
solitude	secrecy	thanksgiving
submission	sacrifice	psalmic
service	study	intercession
confession	worship	
worship	celebration	
guidance	service	
celebration	prayer fellowship	
	intercession	
	submission	

APPENDIX C

THE SEVEN QUESTION METHOD

1. What are you thankful for today?

2. What are you struggling with lately? -or- What is causing stress in your life?

Pray with gratitude and for needs.

Read (don't teach) the Scripture text around the group.

(Texts to explore the whole gospel across Scripture appear on the next page.)

Everyone in group retells the text in their own words while others coach from open Bibles.

3. If this story is from God, what does it teach us about his character? Who is he?

4. If this story is from God, what does it teach us about humanity? What are we really like?

5. If this story is from God, how does it apply to me? or What does God need to change in me? or "I will..."

6. If this story is from God, what should we do together to obey this message from God?

7. Who might you share this story with?

*Genesis 1:1-25	Matthew 3; John 1:29-34
Genesis 2:4-24	Matthew 4:1-11
*Genesis 3:1-13	John 3:1-21
*Genesis 3:14-24	*John 4:1-42
Genesis 6:5-8	Luke 5:17-26
Genesis 6:9-8:14	*Mark 4:35-41
Genesis 8:15-9:17	*Mark 5:1-20
*Genesis 12:1-8	John 11:1-44
Genesis 15:1-6, 17:1-7	Matthew 26:17-30
*Genesis 22:1-19	John 18:1-19:16
Exodus 12:1-28	Luke 23:32-56
*Exodus 20:1-21, Deut. 6.4-5	*Luke 24:1-35
Leviticus 4:1-35	Luke 24:36-53
*Isaiah 53	*John 3:1-21
*Jeremiah 17:5-8	Romans 12.1-2
Habakkuk 3.17-19	1 Corinthians 15:1-11
Luke 1:26-38, 2:1-20	2 Peter 3:5-8
	Revelation 22.1-5

* A list of thirteen texts for a semester length of time.

An electronic version of this tool is available to download from www.kingdomtravelin.com.

APPENDIX D

PRAYING THE SCRIPTURE

Many times, the words of Scripture give us words for prayer. Make a regular discipline of praying the Scripture. These have been found helpful to that end. This list would also be a resource to begin a memorization routine.

Be exalted, O God, above the heavens! Let your glory be over all the earth! Psalms 57:5

For you, O LORD, are most high over all the earth; you are exalted far above all gods. Psalms 97:9

But you, O Lord, are a God merciful and gracious, slow to anger and abounding in steadfast love and faithfulness. Turn to me and be gracious to me; give your strength to your servant, and save the son of your maidservant. Show me a sign of your favor, that those who hate me may see and be put to shame because you, LORD, have helped me and comforted me. Psalms 86:15-17

Not to us, O Lord, not to us, but to your name give glory, for the sake of your steadfast love and your faithfulness! Psalms 115:1

O Lord, our Lord, how majestic is your name in all the earth! Psalm 8:9

Lord, you have been our dwelling place in all generations. Before the mountains were brought forth, or ever you had formed the earth and the world, from everlasting to everlasting you are God. Psalm 90:1-2

I will greatly rejoice in the LORD; my soul shall exult in my God, for he has clothed me with the garments of salvation; he has covered me with the robe of righteousness, … Isaiah 61:10

Let the righteous one rejoice in the LORD and take refuge in him! Let all the upright in heart exult! Psalm 64:10

Come to me, all who labor and are heavy laden, and I will give you rest. Take my yoke upon you, and learn from me, for I am gentle and lowly in heart, and you will find rest for your souls. For my yoke is easy, and my burden is light. Matthew 11:28-30

God is our refuge and strength, a very present help in trouble. Psalm 46:1

The LORD is my light and my salvation; whom shall I fear? The LORD is the stronghold of my life; of whom shall I be afraid? Psalm 27:1

Trust in the LORD with all your heart, and do not lean on your own understanding. Proverbs 3:5

As a father shows compassion to his children, so the LORD shows compassion to those who fear him. For he knows our frame; he remembers that we are dust. Psalm 103:13-14

but whoever listens to me will dwell secure and will be at ease, without dread of disaster. Proverbs 1:33

Stand therefore, having fastened on the belt of truth, and having put on the breastplate of righteousness, and, as shoes for your feet, having put on the readiness given by the gospel of peace. In all circumstances take up the shield of faith, with which you can extinguish all the flaming darts of the evil one; and take the helmet of salvation, and the sword of the Spirit, which is the word of God, praying at all times in the Spirit, with all prayer and supplication. To that end keep alert with all perseverance, making supplication for all the saints,... Ephesians 6:14-18

Bless the LORD, O my soul! O LORD my God, you are very great! You are clothed with splendor and majesty, covering yourself with light as with a garment, stretching out the heavens like a tent. Psalm 104:1-2

Blessed is the man who trusts in the LORD, whose trust is the LORD. He is like a tree planted by water, that sends out its roots by the stream, and does not fear when heat comes, for its leaves remain green, and is not anxious in the year of drought, for it does not cease to bear fruit. Jeremiah 17:7-8

The steadfast love of the LORD never ceases; his mercies never come to an end; they are new every morning; great is your faithfulness. Lamentations 3:22-23

Though the fig tree should not blossom, nor fruit be on the vines, the produce of the olive fail and the fields yield no food, the flock be cut off from the fold and there be no herd in the stalls, yet I will rejoice in the LORD; I will take joy in the God of my salvation. GOD, the Lord, is my strength; he makes my feet like the deer's; he makes me tread on my high places. Habakkuk 3:17-19

...fear not, for I am with you; be not dismayed, for I am your God; I will strengthen you, I will help you, I will uphold you with my righteous right hand. Isaiah 41:10

"Therefore do not be anxious about tomorrow, for tomorrow will be anxious for itself. Sufficient for the day is its own trouble." Matthew 6:34

So we do not lose heart. Though our outer self is wasting away, our inner self is being renewed day by day. For this light momentary affliction is preparing for us an eternal weight of glory beyond all comparison, as we look not to the things that are seen but to the things that are unseen. For the things that are seen are transient, but the things that are unseen are eternal. 2 Corinthians 4:16-18

No, in all these things we are more than conquerors through him who loved us. For I am sure that neither death nor life, nor angels nor rulers, nor things present nor things to come, nor powers, nor height nor depth, nor anything else in all creation, will be able to separate us from the love of God in Christ Jesus our Lord." Romans 8:37-39

Luther urged meditating daily on the Ten Commandments:

You shall have no other gods before me. "You shall not make for yourself a carved image, or any likeness of anything that is in heaven above, or that is in the earth beneath, or that is in the water under the earth. You shall not bow down to them or serve them, for I the LORD your God am a jealous God, visiting the iniquity of the fathers on the children to the third and the fourth generation of those who hate me, but showing steadfast love to thousands of those who love me and keep my commandments.

You shall not take the name of the LORD your God in vain, for the LORD will not hold him guiltless who takes his name in vain.

Remember the Sabbath day, to keep it holy. Six days you shall labor, and do all your work, but the seventh day is a Sabbath to the LORD your God. On it you shall not do any work, you, or your son, or your daughter, your male servant, or your female servant, or your livestock, or the sojourner who is within your gates. For in six days the LORD made heaven and earth, the sea, and all that is in them, and rested on the seventh day. Therefore the LORD blessed the Sabbath day and made it holy.

Honor your father and your mother, that your days may be long in the land that the LORD your God is giving you.

You shall not murder.

You shall not commit adultery.

You shall not steal.

You shall not bear false witness against your neighbor.

You shall not covet your neighbor's house; you shall not covet your neighbor's wife, or his male servant, or his female servant, or his ox, or his donkey, or anything that is your neighbor's. Exodus 20:3-17

APPENDIX E

SELF EVALUATION

The Sailboat Metaphor[1]

Am I Sailing?

Sailing is living the life of a disciple with the Spirit clearly filling my sails. I can feel the reality of God in my heart. I am aware of His presence. I see prayers answered. I can't wait to get into the Scripture and when I do, I hear His voice speaking to me. He shows me through a variety of means that He is working in and through me to bless others. I can't wait to meet with fellow disciples and give Him glory. It is easy to give Him all the glory. I am delighting in Him and through Him.

Am I Rowing?

Rowing means it is more a chore to sit down with God in the morning. I am being faithful to the disciplines of prayer and reading Scripture, but delight seems a memory. I'm wrestling with some doubts and fears and am running to Him and trying to be patient. Even though I know prayers are being answered, I'm not recognizing it. But, no matter what, I will not give up. When I catch myself feeling sorry for myself, I pray some scripture and press on. I'm redoubling my disciplines and letting my fellow disciples know I'm struggling. I may not quite feel it, but I know God is there.

Am I Drifting?

Just like rowing, I'm struggling with doubt and fear, but rather than being disciplined, I've just let go and have sat back in the boat. I'm not only feeling sorry for myself, but I'm keeping it to myself. I've slipped into behaviors that are harmful to me as I seek my identity or fulfilment, not in God, but in my

---

[1] Adapted from: Keller, *Prayer*, p. 258-259.

job, food, sleep, TV, or whatever my favorite attempt at escape maybe. I'm in the shadows and am complacent just sitting here ignoring God. I avoid my fellow disciples, seeing their sin more keenly than I do my own.

Am I Sinking?

I have drifted into the dark. I feel no forward motion in the Christian life. The indifference and doubt has become cynicism, about Scripture, my fellow disciples, even about God. My heart is more stone than flesh. I live in a swirl of self: pity, anger, unforgiveness, criticism and fear. I ignore calls from my fellow disciples and avoid community, seeing their hypocrisy more than my own. Were a tragic event to occur in my life right now, I might walk away from God altogether (in deed if not in word). My negligence has overshadowed my faith in God.

Don't Go It Alone

It's hard to be a disciple alone. Focus on God through prayer and His word. Meet regularly with fellow-disciples. No matter the circumstances, pray no matter what, keep the Scriptures open before you every morning and through the day, meet regularly with fellow-disciples. Row. Row, even if you're pulling the oars and all you see is fog. Just row. Discipline really does lead to delight, so row. Through His word, through prayer and through my fellow-disciples, God will remind me again. The Spirit will blow and I will begin to sail again. God *is* faithful.

But no matter what, row.

An electronic version is available to download at www.kingdomtravelin.com.

APPENDIX F

REGULAR ACCOUNTABILITY

Need Help 1 2 3 4 5 6 7 8 9 Stable

1. How are you doing in the following areas?

consistency in satisfying personal devotions. 1 2 3 4 5 6 7 8 9

battling against ungodly thoughts (unbelief, bitterness, resentment, lust, pride, jealousy, covetousness, racism, etc.) 1 2 3 4 5 6 7 8 9

Your energy for the week ahead. 1 2 3 4 5 6 7 8 9

Your feelings of effectiveness in your pastoral/ministry role. 1 2 3 4 5 6 7 8 9

2. Weekly R&R modules invested: _____ (see bottom of this and next pages)

3. Did you take a day off this past week (three consecutive R&R modules*)? Yes No (If no, how do you plan to compensate for it in the near future?)

4. Have I been with a man or woman in the past week in a way that could be viewed as compromising? Yes No

5. Have any of my financial dealings failed to be filled with integrity? Yes No

6. Have I viewed sexually explicit material? Yes No

7. Have I neglected to give appropriate time to my family? Yes No

8. What would you like me to pray with you about, hold you accountable for or rejoice over (significant stresses, temptations, or joys)?

9. Are you Sailing, Rowing, Drifting or Sinking? Circle the appropriate condition.

10. How is your family joy and harmony? Need Help 1 2 3 4 5 6 7 8 9 Stable

11. Assess your eating & exercise: Unhealthy 1 2 3 4 5 6 7 8 9 Healthy

12. Relationship with your oversight team? Need Help 1 2 3 4 5 6 7 8 9 Stable

I have gratefully adapted this resource from a document created by Bethlehem Baptist Church in Minneapolis, MN. For the purpose of time invested into ministry and time off for rest and family, the pastors split each day into 3 Rest & Rejuvenation (R&R) modules (morning, afternoon, & evening) or 21 modules a week. They have pledged to take off 7-10 R&R modules a week, and to take off 3 of these modules consecutively (to fulfill a Sabbath principle). Below is an example of a week that falls within these guidelines. X is off; W is work.

Leader's Weekly Evaluation of Rest and Work Time

	MON	TUE	WED	THUR	FRI	SAT	SUN
Morning	W	W	W	W	W	X	W
Afternoon	W	W	X	W	W	X	W
Evening	W	W	X	X	X	W	X

In this example, you may see that our leader had a total of 7 R&R modules (off time) as signified by the X Three of them (from Friday evening through Saturday afternoon fulfil the 3 consecutive R&R modules urged here. Thus, according to this model, this leader is being faithful in making time for rest.

Are you?

An electronic version (including a blank form) is available to download at www.kingdomtravelin.com.

APPENDIX G

CONSIDERING BIBLICAL FRUIT

3 His divine power has granted to us all things that pertain to life and godliness, through the knowledge of him who called us to his own glory and excellence, 4 by which he has granted to us his precious and very great promises, so that through them you may become partakers of the divine nature, having escaped from the corruption that is in the world because of sinful desire. 5 For this very reason, make every effort to

supplement your faith with virtue, and

virtue with knowledge, 6 and

knowledge with self-control, and

self-control with steadfastness, and

steadfastness with godliness, 7 and

godliness with brotherly affection, and

brotherly affection with love.

8 For if these qualities are yours and are increasing, they keep you from being ineffective or unfruitful in the knowledge of our Lord Jesus Christ. 9 For whoever lacks these qualities is so nearsighted that he is blind, having forgotten that he was cleansed from his former sins. 10 Therefore, brothers, be all the more diligent to confirm your calling and election, for if you practice these qualities you will never fall. 11 For in this way there will be richly provided for you an entrance into the eternal kingdom of our Lord and Savior Jesus Christ. (2 Peter 1:3-11)

BIBLIOGRAPHY

Allender, Dan. *Sabbath*. Nashville, TN: Thomas Nelson, 2009.

Augustine. Enchiridion on Faith, Hope, and Love. Edited and Translated by Albert Outler. Dallas, TX: Southern Methodist University, 1955. Kindle.

Bagchi, David. "Martin Luther: 'Confessional' Theologian." *Expository Times* Vol. 126(2). Nov. 2014. 53-62.

Barnett, Christopher. *Kierkegaard, Pietism and Holiness*. New York: Routledge, 2011.

Beare, Francis Wright. *The Gospel According to Matthew: A Commentary* Oxford: Blackwell, 1981.

Bauer, Walter, *A Greek-English Lexicon of the New Testament and Other Early Christian Literature,* ed. Frederick W. Danker, 2nd ed. Chicago: University of Chicago Press, 1979.

Beggiani, Seely. *Introduction to Eastern Christian Spirituality: The Syriac Tradition*. London: University of Scranton Press, 1991.

Benedict XVI, *Paul of Tarsus*. London: The Incorporated Catholic Truth Society, 2009.

Blomberg, Craig L. *Matthew: An Exegetical and Theological Exposition of Holy Scripture,* The New American Commentary Series, vol. 23. Nashville, TN: B&H, 1992.

Bonhoeffer, Dietrich. *The Cost of Discipleship*. New York: Simon and Schuster, 1959. Kindle.

Briggs, Alan. *Staying is the New Going*. Colorado Springs, CO: NavPress, 2015. Kindle.

Briggs, J. R. *Fail*. Downer's Grove, IL., InterVarsity, 2014. Kindle.

Broadus, John A. *Commentary on Matthew*. Grand Rapids, MI: Kregel, 1990.

Bruce, A. B. *The Training of the Twelve*. Grand Rapids, MI: Kregel, 1977. Kindle.

Bruce, F. F. *Apostle of the Heart Set Free*. Grand Rapids, MI: Eerdmans, 1977.

Bruner, Frederick Dale. *Matthew: A Commentary*, vol. 2. Grand Rapids, MI: Eerdmans, 1990.

Calvin, John. *Institutes of the Christian Religion.* Edited by John T. McNeill. Translated by Ford Lewis Battles. The Library of Christian Classics, vol. 20. Philadelphia: Westminster Press, 1960.

———. *Commentary on a Harmony of the Evangelists.* vol. 3, Translated by William Pringle. Edinburgh, 1846.

Carson, D. A. *A Call to Spiritual Reformation.* Grand Rapids, MI: Baker, 1992.

Cavarnos, Constantine. "The Functions of Icons" In *Orthodox Christian Information Center,*
http://orthodoxinfo.com/general/icon_function.aspx. (accessed October 23, 2016).

Chambers, Oswald. *My Utmost for His Highest.* New York: Dodd, Mead and Co., 1935; reprint, Westwood, NJ: Barbour and Co., 1963.

Chesterton, Gilbert. K. *What's Wrong with the World.* New York: Dodd, Mead and Co., 1910.

Christian History. "Ignatius of Antioch" In *Christian History* Issue 27 (1990) Carol Stream IL: *Christianity Today,* 1990.
http://www.christianitytoday.com/history/people/martyrs/ignatius-of-antioch.html (accessed May 31, 2016)

Christianity Today. "Still Surprised by Lewis" in *Christianity Today* Vol. 42, No. 10 (September 7, 1998).
http://www.christianitytoday.com/ct/1998/september 7/8ta054.html. (accessed March 4, 2017)

Coleman, Robert. *The Master Plan of Evangelism.* Grand Rapids, MI: Revell, 1993. Kindle.

———. *The Master Plan of Discipleship.* Old Tappan, NJ: Revell, 1987.

Daube, David. *The New Testament and Rabbinic Judaism.* Peabody, MA: Hendrickson, 1956.

———. "Rabbinic Methods of Interpretation and Hellenistic Rhetoric." Hebrew Union College Annual 22 (1949): 239-264. Reprint, *Hebrew Union College.* Edited by D. Philipson. Cincinnati, OH: KTAV, 1968.

de Hamel, Christopher. *The Book. A History of the Bible.* London: Phaidon Press, 2001.

Dunn, James D. G. *Jesus' Call to Discipleship.* New York: Cambridge University Press, 1992.

Early, Dave and Rod Dempsey. *Disciple Making Is.* Nashville, TN: B&H Academic, 2013. Kindle.

Edersheim, Alfred, *The Life and Times of Jesus the Messiah,* Grand Rapids, MI: Eerdmans, 1971.

Egan, Keith. "Discipleship," In HarperCollins Encyclopedia of Catholicism, 1995 edition.

Escobar, Samuel. *The New Global Mission: The Gospel from Everywhere to Everyone.* Downer's Grove, IL: InterVarsity, 2003.

Esler, Ted. "Two Church Planting Paradigms." *International Journal of Frontier Missiology*, 30:2. Summer 2013. 67-73.

Foster, Kenelm, O.P., *The Life of Saint Thomas Aquinas: Biographical Documents.* London: Longmans, Green and Co. 1959.

Foster, Richard. *Celebration of Discipline.* New York, HarperCollins, 1978.

France, R. T. *Matthew*, Tyndale New Testament Commentaries, Grand Rapids, MI: Eerdmans. 1985.

———. *The Gospel of Matthew.* New International Commentary on the New Testament. Grand Rapids, MI: Eerdmans Publishing Co., 2007.

Frend, W. H. C. *The Rise of Christianity*, Philadelphia: Fortress, 1984.

Gonzalez, Justo. *A History of Christian Thought*, vol. 2, Nashville, TN: Abingdon, 1971.

Gorg, Peter. *The Desert Fathers: Anthony and the Beginnings of Monasticism.* Translated by Michael J. Miller. San Francisco: Ignatius, 2011.

Green, Michael. *Matthew for Today: Expository Study of Matthew.* Dallas, TX: Word, 1988.

Gui, Bernard. "Life of St. Thomas Aquinas." In *The Life of Saint Thomas Aquinas: Biographical Documents.* Translated and Edited by Kenelm Foster, O. P. 25-58. London: Longmans, Green and Co. 1959.

Guinness, Os. *The Call: Finding and Fulfilling the Central Purpose of Your Life.* Nashville, TN: Thomas Nelson, 1998. Kindle.

———. *Fool's Talk.* Downers Grove, IL: InterVarsity, 2015. Kindle.

Guthrie, Stan. *Missions in the Third Millennium, 21 Key Trends for the 21st Century.* Waynesboro, GA: Paternoster, 2000.

Hagner, Donald A. *Matthew 14-28*, Word Biblical Commentary Vol. 33a. Dallas, TX: Word Books, 1995.

Hare, Douglas R. A. *Matthew*, Interpretation. Louisville, KY: Westminster John Knox Press, 1993.

Hempton, David. "John Wesley (1703-1791)." In *Pietist Theologians: An Introduction to Theology in the Seventeenth and Eighteenth Centuries.* Edited by Carter Lindberg, 256-272.The Great Theologians. Chichester, GB: Wiley-Blackwell, 2008.

Hendriksen, William. *Exposition of the Gospel According to Matthew*, New Testament Commentary. Grand Rapids, MI: Baker, 1973.

Hulse, Erroll and David Kingdon, Editors. *A Marvelous Ministry: How the All-round Ministry of Charles Haddon Spurgeon Speaks to Us Today.* Grand Rapids, MI: Soli Deo Gloria, 1993.

Hummel, Charles. *Tyranny of the Urgent.* Downer's Grove, IL, InterVarsity, 1967.

Jacobitz, Gerard, "The Epistolary Correspondence of Saints Jerome and Augustine and the Expansion of the Rule of Saint Benedict from 66 to 73 Chapters" in *American Benedictine Review* 63, no. 4 (Dec 2012).

Jenkins, Philip. *The Next Christendom: The Coming of Global Christianity.* New York: Oxford University Press, 2011. Kindle.

Keller, Timothy. *Prayer: Experiencing Awe and Intimacy with God.* New York: Dutton, 2014. Kindle.

———. *Preaching.* New York: Viking, 2015. Kindle.

à Kempis, Thomas. *The Imitation of Christ. Translated by* William Creasy. Notre Dame, IN: Ave Maria, 1989.

Lawrence. *The Practice of the Presence of God.* Translated by John J. Delaney. New York: Image, 1977.

Lewis, C. S. *Mere Christianity.* New York: Macmillan, 1952; Reprint, New York: HarperCollins, 2009. Kindle.

———. *The Collected Letters of C. S. Lewis Vol. I: Family Letters 1905-1931.* Edited by Walter Hooper. New York: HarperSanFrancisco, 2004.

———. *The Collected Letters of C. S. Lewis Vol. II: Books, Broadcasts, and the War 1931-1949.* Edited by Walter Hooper. New York: HarperSanFrancisco, 2004.

———. *Four Loves.* London, Bles, 1960. Reprint, New York: Inspirational Press, 1987.

———. *The Weight of Glory.* 1949. Reprint, Grand Rapids, MI: Eerdmans, 1979.

Lieberman, Saul. *Hellenism in Jewish Palestine.* New York: Jewish Theological Seminary, 1962.

Lindberg, Carter. *Pietist Theologians: An Introduction to Theology in the Seventeenth and Eighteenth Centuries.* The Great Theologians. Chichester, GB: Wiley-Blackwell, 2008.

Luther, Martin. *A Simple Way to Pray.* Translated by C. Harrison. St. Louis, MO: Concordia, 2012. Kindle.

———. *Word and Sacrament.* Luther's Works Vol. 38, Translated and Edited by Helmut Lehmann and Martin Lehmann. Saint Louis, MO: Concordia,1958.

Luz, Ulrich. *Matthew 21-28, A Commentary*. Minneapolis, MN: Augsburg Fortress, 2005.

McGrath, Alister. *C. S. Lewis - A Life: Eccentric Genius, Reluctant Prophet*. Carol Stream, IL: Tyndale House, 2013. Kindle.

Meye, Robert. *Jesus and the Twelve: Discipleship and Revelation in Mark's Gospel*. Grand Rapids, MI: Eerdmans, 1968.

Morris, Leon. *The Gospel According to Matthew*. Pillar New Testament Commentary. Grand Rapids, MI: Eerdmans, 1992.

Mounce, Robert H. *Matthew*. New International Biblical Commentary. Edited by Robert K. Johnston, W. Ward Gasque, Robert L. Hubbard, Jr. Peabody, MA: Hendrickson, 1985.

Nassif, Bradley. "Are Eastern Orthodoxy and Evangelicalism Compatible? Yes." In *Three Views on Eastern Orthodoxy and Evangelicalism*, Edited by James Stamoolis, 26-88. Counterpoints: Exploring Theology. Grand Rapids, MI: Zondervan, 2004.

Neusner, Jacob. *There We Sat Down: Talmudic Judaism in the Making*. Nashville, TN: Abingdon, 1971.

———. *Judaism in the Beginning of Christianity*. Philadelphia: Fortress, 1984.

———. "The Figure of Hillel" In *Judaism in the Beginning of Christianity* Philadelphia: Fortress, 1984.

Newbigin, Lesslie. *Proper Confidence: Faith, Doubt, and Certainty in Christian Discipleship*. Grand Rapids, MI: Publishing, 1995.

Nouwen, Henri J. M. *Behold the Beauty of the Lord*. Notre Dame, IN: Ave Maria, 1987.

Olson, Roger. *The Story of Christian Theology*. Downers Grove, IL: InterVarsity, 1999.

Ozment, Steven E. "Homo Spiritualis: A Comparative study of the Anthropology of Johannes Tauler, Jean Gerson and Martin Luther (1509-16) in the Context of their Theological Thought" in *Studies in Medieval and Reformation Thought*, Vol. 6. Edited by Heiko Oberman. Leiden, GY: E. J. Brill, 1969.

———. "An Aid to Luther's Marginal Comments on Johannes Tauler's Sermons." In *Harvard Theological Review* Vol. 63, No. 2 (April, 1970). http://www.jstor.org/stable/1509029 (accessed 12 June 2016).

Packer, J. I., *Knowing God*. Downer's Grove, IL: InterVarsity, 1973.

Pierson, Arthur T. *George Mueller of Bristol and His Witness to A Prayer-Hearing God*. Grand Rapids, MI: Kregel, 1999.

Pope, Randy, *Insourcing*. Grand Rapids, MI: Zondervan, 2013.

Rengstorf, K. H. "mathánō." In *Theological Dictionary of the New Testament*, Edited by Gerhard Kittel and Gerhard Friedrich. Translated, Edited and Abridged by Geoffrey W. Bromiley. Grand Rapids, MI: Eerdmans, 1985.

Robertson, A. T. *A Harmony of the Gospels for Students of the Life of Christ*. New York: Harpers and Row, 1922.

Sayer, George. *Jack: A Life of C. S. Lewis*. Wheaton, IL: Crossway, 1988.

Schnackenburg, Rudolf. *The Gospel of Matthew*. Translated by Robert R. Barr. Grand Rapids, MI: Eerdmans, 2002.

Scott, Alan. *Plato's Socrates as Educator*. Albany, NY: State University Press, 2000.

Scazerro, Peter. *Emotionally Healthy Spirituality*. Grand Rapids, MI: Zondervan, 2006.

Smith, David. *The Life and Letters of St. Paul*. New York: G. H. Doran, 1923.

Spener, Philip Jacob. *Pia Desideria*. Translated and Edited by Theodore Tappert. Minneapolis, MN: Fortress Press, 1964.

Staniloae, Dumitru. *Orthodox Spirituality*. Translated by Archimandrite Jerome and Otilia Kloos. South Canaan, PA: St. Tikhon's Orthodox Theological Seminary Press, 2002.

Stoeffler, F. Ernest. *German Pietism During the Eighteenth Century*. Leiden, Netherlands: E.J. Brill, 1973.

———. *The Rise of Evangelical Pietism*. Leiden, Netherlands: E.J. Brill, 1971.

Stott, John. *The Radical Disciple: Some Neglected Aspects of Our Calling*. Downers Grove, IL: InterVarsityPress, 2012. Kindle edition.

St. Theophan the Recluse. *The Path to Salvation*. Safford, AZ: St. Paisius Monastery, 2006.

Torrell, Jean-Pierre, O.P., *Saint Thomas Aquinas*, Vol. 1, *The Person and His Work*. Translated by Robert Royal. Washington D.C.: Catholic University of America Press, 1996.

———. *Saint Thomas Aquinas*, Vol. 2, *Spiritual Master*. Translated by Robert Royal. Washington D.C.: Catholic University of America Press, 2003.

———. *Christ and Spirituality in St. Thomas Aquinas*. Translated by Bernard Blankenhorn. Washington D.C.: Catholic University of America Press, 2011.

Toumanova, Nina A. trans. "The Way of a Pilgrim," In *A Treasury of Russian Spirituality*. Edited by G. P. Fedotov. 1965; Reprint, Mineola, NY: Dover Publications, 2003.

Vlastos, Gregory. "The Socratic Elenchus: Method is All." *Socratic Studies.* *Edited by* Myles Burnyeat. New York: Cambridge University Press, 1994.

Ward, Benedicta. *The Desert Fathers: Sayings of the Early Christian Monks.* London: Penguin Books, 2003. Kindle.

Webber, Robert. *The Divine Embrace.* Grand Rapids, MI: Baker Books, 2006.

Wilkins, Michael J. *Following the Master: A Biblical Theology of Discipleship.* Grand Rapids, MI: Zondervan, 1992.

Willard, Dallas. *Renovation of the Heart.* Colorado Springs, CO: NavPress, 2002.

———. *The Great Omission.* New York: HarperCollins, 2006.

———. *Spirit of the Disciplines.* New York: HarperCollins, 1988.

Young, Brad. *Meet the Rabbis: Rabbinic Thought and the Teachings of Jesus.* Peabody, MA: Hendrickson, 2007.

INDEX

ABOUT THE AUTHOR

Thomas (Tom) Foley is married to Anna and they have two married daughters, and are proud grandparents. He is a graduate of Liberty University (B.S.), Liberty Baptist Theological Seminary; (M.A.R.) and Gordon-Conwell Theological Seminary (D. Min.). He is a founder and is Executive Director of Christian Educators Outreach of Charlottesville, Virginia. Tom travels internationally in a pastoral role serving pastors, missionaries and Christian leaders. After military service and 20 years in the business world, Tom has been a youth pastor, pastor, Bible teacher and private school chaplain. He is now the Executive Director of Christian Educators Outreach. He is a frequent blogger at www.kingdomtravelin.com, tweets at @revtomtravels, and is on LinkedIn. When he's not on a train or plane, he is at home with Anna in Charlottesville.

There are more resources in the works: on leadership; on the five big ideas from the Reformation and why they matter in our personal discipleship and a devotional guide based on the M'Cheyne reading plan.

If you would like to have Tom speak to your group, church or organization about congregation based disciple making, missions or his travels in the kingdom, his contact info is at www.ceokids.org.

ABOUT CHRISTIAN EDUCATORS OUTREACH

This book is a ministry resource that is published by CEO to provide training, provoke thought and engage conversations about disciple making. The views expressed in *As We're Going* are those of the author and not necessarily those of Christian Educators Outreach, its Board of Directors or its employees.

Christian Educators Outreach (CEO) is a not-for-profit, 501(c)(3) organization formed in the USA for spreading of the gospel of Jesus Christ through the support of partner organizations. We Are Extending Gospel Partnerships Worldwide through Identifying, Training and Mentoring Leaders.

As a not-for-profit organization, CEO relies on contributions that are solicited and received with the understanding that Christian Educators Outreach has complete control over the use of donated funds and will be used for our mission.

Christian Educators Outreach
P.O. Box 6578
Charlottesville VA
22906

CEO is qualified to receive tax deductible donations. CEO works to maintain transparency in our affairs. We report regularly to our board of directors; our finances are reviewed annually by an independent CPA firm and finances are submitted to an annual accreditation review by the Evangelical Council for Financial Accountability.

There's more about our work, serving abroad with us, or joining us in financial partnership on our website: www.ceokids.org.

www.ingramcontent.com/pod-product-compliance
Lightning Source LLC
Chambersburg PA
CBHW071531040426
42452CB00008B/972